DECORATIVE
ART
and Modern Interiors

DECORATIVE ART

and Modern Interiors 1974/75

Volume 64
edited by Maria Schofield

A Studio Book
The Viking Press · New York

Cover
Country Home at Goodleigh, England
Architects Aldington & Craig
Photography by Richard Einzig

Title Page
SAORI lighting modules designed by
Kazuhide Takahama for Sirrah srl, Italy
(enlarged photograph)

Published in London by Studio Vista
a division of
Cassell & Collier Macmillan Publishers Ltd,
35 Red Lion Square, London WC1R 4SG
an affiliate of Macmillan Inc, New York
Copyright © Studio Vista 1974
Designed by Keith Kail
Published in New York by The Viking Press, Inc.
625 Madison Avenue, New York, N.Y. 10022
ISBN 0 289 70462 6
US SBN 670-26278-1
Library of Congress catalog card number 74-464
Printed in Great Britain
by Colour Reproductions Ltd, Billericay
and bound by R. J. Acfords Ltd, Chichester

Contents

Acknowledgments

The Editor wishes to thank those manufacturers and designers who supplied photographs for reproduction and especially the following contributors who waived reproduction rights and/or lent illustrations:

Sergio Asti
Carla Caccia
The Crafts Advisory Council of Great Britain
Foster Associates
Hellmuth, Obata & Kassabaum Architects
Interlübke Möbelfabrik
Hans-Agne Jakobsson
Kisho N Kurokawa
Landes Manufacturing Co
Minale, Tattersfield, Provinciali
Ico and Luisa Parisi
F O Peterson & Söner Byggnads AB
Renwick Gallery, National Collection of Fine Arts, Smithsonian Institution
Royal Leerdam Glassworks
Wiese Vitsoe

Introduction

To a reader unfamiliar with the tradition of *DECORATIVE ART*, the opening features of this year's edition might suggest that the book follows primarily the interests of architect or planner, rather than those of the interior designer. Over the years this annual has offered a meeting ground to all those concerned with life environments, but this issue has been planned in the conviction that a better practice of design could be achieved by a closer integration between exterior and interior architecture, especially considering how often the actual shape of rooms is determined by the structural problems of an architectural complex. The editor believes further that the particular atmosphere surrounding a building should inspire and direct the work of the interior designer, and the talented photographers who have worked for this edition have set out to capture some of this intangible quality. The present stage of development of the Barbican complex in the City of London and the innovative work done in Japan by Kisho N Kurokawa, an already well-known architect and planner not yet in his forties, illustrate this approach. A belief in integration in other aspects of decorative art has influenced later sections of this issue.

Of the twenty interiors included in this book seven belong to public buildings, including hotels, offices, shops and schools. Here the intention is to demonstrate the widening of scope in interior design when the brief concerns the needs of an occupant who carries out a specialized activity. Work in this public domain often attracts resources and techniques not yet available for private ventures. The most advanced and sophisticated devices made available by technology, the combined use of traditional and new materials, the graphic virtuosity of an artist, are only a few examples of the many ways of achieving an active relationship between designer and user.

The choice of domestic interiors proposes a variety of solutions to the task of matching the designer's vision to the customer's requirements. In two cases, the Family Holiday Home at Montorfano and the Antidwelling Box, the architects were able to plan both building and furnishing: the results, though possibly controversial, are undeniably striking. The eleven remaining features deal with city apartments, homes with a country outlook, homes and workshops of designers, and finally conversions, that ever appealing task of creating a modern home out of an existing building often designed with a quite different use in mind.

The special feature on Glass represents a new venture for *DECORATIVE ART*. Within the limited scope of a year book it has never been possible to cover all aspects of world production in the fields of decorative craft and industry. By directing research to a different subject each issue, it is hoped to provide the reader with a collection of factual, mainly visual, information complemented by the views of people whose work is related to the subject being treated in some depth. On the present occasion Otto Wittmann and Robert F Phillips, of the Toledo Museum of Art, and Michael Robinson, of the Ulster Museum in Belfast, give their accounts of the International and the American scene in Glass development, as an industry and as an art. Otto Wittmann and Robert F Phillips were jointly responsible for the organization of the exhibition *AMERICAN GLASS NOW* which has been seen by a large audience in the United States through the participation of other museums over the last two years. Michael Robinson is associated with the work done at the Department of Fine Arts of the Ulster Museum, which includes lecturing and organizing exhibitions. All three are contributing to the growing interest in the revival of this fascinating craft.

A selection of ceramic objects has been included to record in *DECORATIVE ART* the tendency among a younger generation of ceramicists, such as Alessio Tasca and Jacqueline Poncelet, to make use of mechanical aids and industrial methods for the production of art pieces; this is happening today, concurrently with the practice of traditional hand-throwing techniques which culminates with the inspiring work of Lucie Rie or of Gertrud and Otto Natzler.

To illustrate trends noticed in the contemporary furnishing style, designs of furniture, lighting, textiles are shown together on the same page. This has been done to give more relevance to the characteristics of particular items, not to suggest how to design room settings. At times editor and designer were guided by the presence of some affinity they could sense between certain designs, in other cases they purposely set the chosen subjects against each other, so that their visual impact could be heightened by contrast.

There could be no end to the observation of many exciting developments in the activity of our contributors. If the examples illustrated in this book could establish yet another link between the artist and the reader, a most ambitious aim would then have been achieved.

Maria Schofield

Einführung

Dem Leser, dem die Tradition von *DECORATIVE ART* unbekannt ist, könnte es nach Lesen der ersten Artikel in der diesjährigen Auflage erscheinen, daß dieses Buch hauptsächlich an den Architekten oder Planer gerichtet ist und nicht so sehr an den Innenarchitekten. Im Laufe der Jahre ist das Jahrbuch zum Treffpunkt aller derjenigen geworden, die sich mit unserer Umwelt befassen. Diese Ausgabe wurde jedoch mit der Überzeugung geschaffen, daß eine bessere Formgebung durch engere Integration zwischen Außen- und Innenarchitektur möglich sein könnte, besonders wenn man überlegt, wie oft die eigentliche Form eines Zimmers von den Bauproblemen eines architektonischen Komplexes bestimmt wird. Der Herausgeber glaubt ferner, daß die Atmosphäre, die ein Gebäude umgibt, den Innenarchitekten anregen und leiten sollte. Die begabten Fotografen, die wir für diese Ausgabe eingesetzt haben, haben versucht, etwas von dieser unerklärlichen Qualität einzufangen. Das derzeitige Baustadium des Barbican-Komplexes in London und die neuartigen Arbeiten, die Kisho N Kurokawa, ein bereits gut bekannter Architekt und Planer, in Japan zeigte, obwohl er noch nicht das reife Alter von 40 erreicht hat, sind ein Beispiel für diese Möglichkeit. Der Glaube an eine Integration auf anderen Gebieten der Innenarchitektur hat spätere Teile dieser Ausgabe beeinflußt.

Von den zwanzig Innengestaltungen, die dieses Buch zeigt, stammen sieben aus öffentlichen Gebäuden wie Hotels, Büros, Läden und Schulen. Hier war beabsichtigt, den erweiterten Gesichtskreis in der Innenarchitektur zu zeigen, wenn das Pflichtenheft die Bedürfnisse eines Bewohners angibt, der eine spezifische Tätigkeit ausübt. Die Arbeit auf diesem öffentlichen Gebiet zieht oft Möglichkeiten und Verfahren heran, die privaten Unternehmen noch nicht zur Verfügung stehen. Die modernsten und höchstentwickelten Vorrichtungen, die durch die Technik zur Verfügung stehen, die Kombination traditioneller und neuer Materialien, die gestalterische Virtuosität eines Künstlers sind nur einige wenige Beispiele für die vielen Möglichkeiten, eine aktive Beziehung zwischen Innenarchitekt und Benutzer zu erzielen.

Bei der Wahl der Raumgestaltung bieten sich mehrere Möglichkeiten, die Ansichten des Innenarchitekten mit dem Bedarf des Kunden auf einen Nenner zu bringen. In zwei Fällen, einem Ferienhaus einer Familie in Montorfano und dem 'Antiwohnkasten', konnten die Architekten sowohl das Gebäude wie auch die Einrichtung planen. Auch wenn die Ergebnisse möglicherweise widersprüchlich sind, sind sie zweifellos verblüffend. Die elf restlichen Bilder sind Stadtwohnungen, Privathäuser mit Sicht auf das Land, Privathäuser und Werkstätten von Innenarchitekten und schließlich umgebaute Häuser, bei denen man die ansprechende Aufgabe wahrnehmen kann, aus einem bereits vorhandenen Gebäude, das oft für einen ganz anderen Zweck bestimmt war, ein modernes Heim zu schaffen.

Der Sonderartikel über Glas ist ein neues Unternehmen für *DECORATIVE ART*. In dem beschränkten Bereich eines Jahrbuches war es noch nie möglich, alle Aspekte der Weltproduktion auf dem Gebiet von Innendekoration und Industrie zu behandeln. Indem wir unsere Untersuchungen in jeder Ausgabe auf ein anderes Thema lenken, hoffen wir, dem Leser eine Sammlung aktueller, hauptsächlich visueller Informationen zu liefern, und zusätzlich die Ansichten von Leuten, deren Arbeit sich mit dem behandelten Thema in einer gewissen Tiefe befaßt. Dieses Mal behandeln Otto Wittmann und Robert F Phillips aus dem Kunstmuseum Toledo und Michael Robinson vom Ulster-Museum in Belfast Glas in Bezug auf seinen internationalen Einsatz und in Amerika als Industrie und Kunstrichtung. Otto Wittman und Robert F Phillips waren für die Organisation einer Ausstellung unter dem Titel *AMERICAN GLASS NOW* verantwortlich, die in den Vereinigten Staaten eine große Besucherzahl anzog, da auch andere Museen in den letzten zwei Jahren teilnahmen. Michael Robinson ist mit den Arbeiten der Abteilung für schöne Künste des Ulster-Museums verbunden, einschließlich Vorlesungen und der Organisation von Ausstellungen. Alle drei tragen zum wachsenden Interesse an der Wiederauferstehung dieses faszinierenden Handwerks bei.

Eine Sammlung von Keramiken wurde ebenfalls eingeschlossen, um in *DECORATIVE ART* festzustellen, daß eine Tendenz bei der jüngeren Generation der Keramiker besteht, wie Alessio Tasca und Jacqueline Poncelet, sich mechanische Hilfsmittel und industrielle Methoden zur Herstellung von Kunstwerken zunutze machen. Das geschieht heute neben der Anwendung traditioneller Handformverfahren, was in der anregenden Arbeit von Lucie Rie oder Gertrud und Otto Natzler gipfelt.

Um die beobachteten Trends in modernen Möbelstil zu zeigen, erscheinen auch auf der gleichen Seite Muster, Möbel, Lampen, Textilien. Das wurde getan, damit die Eigenschaften der einzelnen gezeigten Gegenstände mehr Bezugskraft erhielten, nicht um die Einrichtung eines Zimmers vorzuschreiben. Von Zeit zu Zeit ließen sich Herausgeber und Innenarchitekt durch das Vorhandensein einer gewissen Verwandtschaft zwischen gewissen Einrichtungen leiten, in anderen Fällen ließen sie willkürlich gewisse Themen mit einander kontrastieren, so daß ihre Durchschlagskraft durch den Kontrast noch erhöht wurde.

Die Beobachtung der vielen interessanten Entwicklungen in der Tätigkeit derjenigen, die uns Beiträge liefern, hat kein Ende. Wenn die in diesem Buch gezeigten Beispiele eine weitere Verbindung zwischen Künstler und Leser herstellen, dann ist unser Ziel schon erreicht.

Maria Schofield

Introducción

Para el lector que desconozca la tradición de *DECORATIVE ART*, los reportajes que abren la edición de este año tal vez le hagan pensar que se trata de una publicación destinada al arquitecto o al urbanizador antes que al realizador de interiores. En realidad, durante el curso de los años este anuario ha venido constituyendo una tribuna a la que acuden todos los que tienen algo que ver con el medio ambiente vital; pero la presente edición parte del criterio de que una coloboración más estrecha entre arquitectura exterior e interior permitiría alcanzar mejores normas de ejecución, máxime teniendo en cuenta que, en muchos casos, la forma efectiva de una habitación viene determinada por los problemas estructurales de un complejo arquitectónico. El Director considera, además, que el ambiente que rodea a un determinado edificio debe inspirar y encauzar la labor desempeñada por el realizador de interiores, lo que ha servido de acicate para que nuestros perspicaces fotógrafos capten algo de esta cualidad intangible. Tal enfoque queda ilustrado por la etapa de desarrollo actual del polígono 'Barbican' en la City de Londres y por los trabajos innovadores que en el Japón ha llevado a cabo Kisho N Kurokawa, arquitecto y urbanizador que, sin haber cumplido aún los cuarenta años, goza ya de fama internacional. En otras secciones del presente número se preconiza la integración de diversos aspectos del arte decorativo.

De los veinte interiores que figuran en este libro siete corresponden a edificios públicos, entre ellos hoteles, oficinas, comercios y escuelas. Se trata con ello de demostrar las amplias posibilidades que brinda el diseño interior de un local cuyo ocupante se dedica a una actividad especializada. A veces, la intervención en este sector público atrae recursos y técnicas que todavía no se hallan a disposición de la empresa privada. Las soluciones más avanzadas y complejas que ha proporcionado la tecnología, la combinación de materiales nuevos y tradicionales, la virtuosidad propia de un artista, constituyen sólo unos pocos ejemplos de las muchas formas en que se puede establecer una relación activa entre realizador y usuario.

Los diversos interiores domésticos elegidos proponen una variedad de soluciones al problema de combinar la visión del realizador con las necesidades del cliente. En dos casos: la 'casa de verano familiar' de Montorfano y la llamada 'caja antimoradora', los arquitectos han concebido tanto el inmueble como el mobiliario. El resultado, aunque tal vez no guste a todos, no deja de ser impresionante. Los otros once artículos se ocupan de los apartamentos urbanos, viviendas con aspecto rural, los domicilios y talleres de los propios realizadores y, por último, la conversión: esa siempre interesante tarea de crear un hogar moderno partiendo de un edificio ideado, en muchos casos, con un fin totalmente distinto.

Con su reportaje monográfico sobre el Vidrio, *DECORATIVE ART* cobra un nuevo rumbo. En efecto, nunca ha sido posible, dentro del limitado alcance de un anuario, abarcar todos los aspectos de la producción mundial en los campos artesanal e industrial de la decoración. Al encauzar las investigaciones hacia un tópico distinto en cada edición, se intenta presentar al lector un conjunto de datos fácticos, en su mayor parte visuales, complementados por el criterio de personas cuya labor está relacionada con el tema así destacado. En esta ocasión, Otto Wittmann y Robert F Phillips, del Museo de Arte de Toledo (Estados Unidos) y Michael Robinson del Museo del Ulster, de Belfast, exponen el panorama internacional y norteamericano del Vidrio, en cuanto industria y en cuanto arte. Otto Wittmann y Robert F Phillips fueron los organizadores de la exposición *'AMERICAN GLASS NOW'* que durante los dos últimos años ha sido presenciada por un nutrido público en los Estados Unidos, gracias a la colaboración prestada por otros museos del país. Por su parte, Michael Robinson está vinculado al Departamento de Bellas Artes del Museo del Ulster, dedicándose a pronunciar conferencias y a la organización de certámenes. Los tres citados contribuyen así al creciente interés por el restablecimiento de tan apasionante arte.

Se ha incluido una selección de objetos de cerámica, a fin de dejar constancia en *DECORATIVE ART* de la tendencia de la joven generación de ceramistas, entre los que se cuentan Alessio Tasca y Jacqueline Poncelot, a producir objetos de arte valiéndose de ayudas mecánicas y métodos industriales. Esta práctica de hoy, en combinación con el tradicional torneado a mano, encuentra su punto culminante en la inspirada obra de Lucie Rie o de Gertrud y Otto Natzler.

Para ilustrar las tendencias de estilo observadas en el mobiliario contemporáneo, se exponen en una misma página ejemplos de muebles, alumbrado y textiles, habiéndose hecho así, no con el propósito de indicar los conjuntos que mejor le van a un cuarto, sino para realzar las características individuales de los elementos ilustrados. A veces, el Director y el realizador se guiaban por una afinidad que habían percibido entre ciertos diseños; en otros casos, procedieron intencionadamente a confrontar entre sí los artículos elegidos, a fin de que el contraste intensificara su impacto visual.

No tiene fin la observación de las interesantes novedades que informan la actividad de nuestros colaboradores. Si los ejemplos que figuran en este libro tuvieran el efecto de forjar aún otro vínculo entre el artista y el lector, se habría alcanzado por fin un objetivo muy codiciado.

Maria Schofield

Introduction

Un lecteur qui connait mal les traditions de *DECORATIVE ART* pourrait croire, en lisant les articles de tête de l'édition de cette année, que l'ouvrage intéresse surtout l'architecte ou ceux qui sont chargés de dresser les plans plutôt que le décorateur d'intérieur. Au fil des ans, cet annuaire s'est présenté comme le point de ralliement de tous ceux qui se préoccupent du cadre et de l'environnement de l'existence, mais cette année, il a été composé avec la conviction qu'on améliorerait les projets en recherchant une intégration plus complète des architectures intérieure et extérieure, et cela surtout si l'on considère à quel point il est fréquent que la forme même des pièces soit déterminée par la structure d'un ensemble architectural. Le directeur de cette publication pense, en outre, que l'atmosphère particulière qu'enveloppe un édifice devrait inspirer et orienter le travail du décorateur d'intérieur. Les photographes de talent qui ont travaillé pour cette édition se sont efforcés de saisir cette harmonie subtile. Citons, pour illustrer cette approche, l'aspect actuel du grand ensemble de Barbican, dans la Cité de Londres, et le travail de pionnier accompli au Japon par Kisho N Kurokawa, architecte et maître d'oeuvre déjà très connu, bien qu'il n'ait pas encore atteint la quarantaine. Une certaine foi dans la possibilité d'intégrer d'autres éléments de l'art décoratif a guidé le choix d'une partie des titres de cet ouvrage.

Sur les vingt intérieurs présentés dans ce volume, sept sont ceux d'édifices ouverts au public — hôtels, bureaux, magasins ou écoles. L'objectif, ici, est de démontrer que l'apport de la decoration d'intérieur est d'autant plus riche qu'il tient mieux compte des besoins d'un occupant qui exerce une activité spécialisée. Lorsqu'il s'agit de lieux publics on peut souvent utiliser des ressources et des techniques qui ne trouvent pas encore une place ailleurs. Les moyens les plus avancés et les plus sophistiqués, l'emploi combiné de matériaux traditionnels et nouveaux, la virtuosité graphique d'un artiste, sont des exemples des très nombreuses façons d'assurer une liaison meilleure entre le concepteur et l'utilisateur.

Pour les intérieurs privés, le choix a porté sur diverses solutions du problème posé par l'harmonisation des idées du décorateur et les besoins du client. Dans deux cas — la Maison Familiale de Vacances à Montorfano et le Box Antihabitacle — les architectes furent à même d'élaborer le bâtiment et le mobilier; les résultats sont peut-être discutables, mais incontestablement frappants. Les onze autres présentations portent sur des appartements en ville, sur des logis aux vues campagnardes, sur des foyers et ateliers de décorateurs, et, pour finir, sur des transformations, entreprises toujours attrayantes où la création d'un intérieur moderne tire parti d'un bâtiment existant, bien souvent conçu en vue d'une tout autre destination.

La rubrique spéciale consacrée au Verre est une innovation pour *DECORATIVE ART*. Les dimensions limitées d'un annuaire n'ont jamais permis de traiter de tous les aspects de la production mondiale des arts décoratifs et des industries qui s'y rattachent. En axant les investigations sur un sujet différent chaque fois, on espère fournir au lecteur un ensemble de documentation principalement visuelle, que complètent les opinions de personnalités dont les travaux touchent au sujet qui fait l'objet d'une étude approfondie. En cette occasion, Otto Wittmann et Robert F Phillips, du Toledo Museum of Art, ainsi que Michael Robinson, de l'Ulster Museum de Belfast, exposent leurs vues sur les activités mondiales et notamment américaines dans le domaine du Verre, considéré à la fois comme une industrie et comme un art. Otto Wittmann et Robert F Phillips ont assumé l'organisation de l'exposition *AMERICAN GLASS NOW* qui a reçu, ces deux dernières années, de très nombreux visiteurs aux Etats-Unis grâce au concours d'autres musées. Michael Robinson contribue, par des conférences et des organisations d'expositions, aux travaux de la branche 'Beaux Arts' de l'Ulster Museum. Tous trois sont pour beaucoup dans l'intérêt croissant que suscite la renaissance de ces fascinants métiers d'art.

Un choix d'objets en céramique a été ajouté afin de marquer dans *DECORATIVE ART* la tendance, dans la jeune génération des spécialistes, tels qu'Alessio Tasca et Jacqueline Poncelet, à recourir, pour produire des oeuvres d'art, à l'appoint de procédés mécaniques et à des méthodes industrielles. La chose se pratique aujourd'hui, concurremment aux pratiques traditionnelles de tournage manuel qui atteignent leur suprême expression dans les oeuvres exaltantes de Lucie Rie ou de Gertrud et Otto Natzler.

Pour illustrer les tendances qui se remarquent dans le style contemporain du mobilier, des modèles de meubles, d'éclairage et de tissus sont présentés dans une même page. Ce groupement a pour but de conférer plus d'importance aux caractéristiques des articles, mais nullement de suggérer comment concevoir la décoration des pièces. En certaines occasions le directeur de la publication et le modéliste se sont laissés guider par les affinités que leur semblaient présenter certains modèles, mais dans d'autres cas, ils ont à dessein créé une opposition entre les objets choisis, pour que l'impact visuel soit accentué par le contraste.

On pourrait s'étendre longuement sur les stimulantes réalisations des artistes cités dans cette édition. Si les exemples qui illustrent ce livre pouvaient établir un lien de plus entre artiste et lecteur, un objectif des plus ambitieux se trouverait atteint.

Maria Schofield

City development
and
Private dwellings

The Barbican Complex, London

Architects
Chamberlin Powell & Bon
Photography by Sam Sawdon,
Richard Einzig, John Maltby

Conceived as an architectural complex of heroic proportions, on a site made available by the bombing of the City of London during World War II, the planning of the Barbican as a residential area has been conducted in full awareness that this was also a unique occasion for creating a cultural centre within the most ancient part of a great city, near one of the world's most established business institutions.

At the present stage of development, its powerful structures are pervaded by an atmosphere of strength and beauty. The remains of the Roman Wall and the Church of St Giles, testimony

2 Remains of the Roman Wall among new office blocks in the City of London

of great ages of the past, have been lovingly restored and surrounded by flowing water and open spaces. The banks of water basins, graced by waterlilies, are studded with old tombstones from St Giles' destroyed churchyard, and young girls attending the City of London School stroll among ancient columns at break time. No motor traffic is possible at pedestrian level, and the sound of water cascading into the lake overcomes at times the noise of traffic from the nearby streets, becoming more prominent as the day's activity ceases.

3 St Giles Church and the
Barbican Towers; on the
foreground the Roman Wall
Photography Sam Sawdon

4 One of the residential towers; Victorian street lamps have been retained.
Photography John Maltby Ltd

5 Entrance to underground parking (right). On the left, view over gardens; in the foreground, communal area and passage from where motor traffic is excluded.
Photography Richard Einzig

7 *Overpage*
An overall view of the lake
as reflected in a town-house
window in the Barbican.
*Photography Richard
Einzig*

This particular atmosphere attracts many people to live in the
Barbican and will probably be the basis for the establishment of
a real community once the scheme is completed and the Arts
Centre in full activity. Today one can only record the examples
of individuality in the furnishing of homes by people who are
already living there.

The living room of a one-bedroom flat (below, Fig. 6) contains numerous objects and rugs collected by the owners during
their travels; here Japanese lamps, Mexican hangings, and bark
paintings contibute to give the place an exotic and festive look.

In the two-bedroom house illustrated on page 22, red pin-
board and white shelving cover one wall of the entrance hall, a
landing-type passage leading to two bedrooms and the bathroom; from the hall an elegant spiral staircase leads down to
the living/dining room and adjoining kitchen. The furnishing here
is in calm, cool tones of oatmeal, white and green, but over the
entire wall of the stairwell there is a huge hanging in bold checks
of orange and pink which unifies the two floors and provides a
contrast to the more restrained mood of the living room.

6 One of the garden flats:
living/dining room.
Photography Sam Sawdon

8 A two-bedroom house:
Entrance

9 Bedroom

10 Living/Dining Room

11 Living Area

Photography Sam Sawdon

The BC25 Capsule, Japan

Architect Kisho N Kurokawa

This is an example of 'system building' at its most practical in a densely populated metropolis, intended to meet needs related to the normal running of everyday life, albeit a privileged, highly organized life.

The brief here was to build a 'businessman's hotel' in Ginza, one of Tokyo's most fashionable districts. The solution took the shape of two towers of steel and reinforced concrete, centred on a 'platform' composed of two floors and a basement. The basement is entirely occupied by a machine room, the ground floor consists of entrance hall and restaurant, and the first floor functions as an office, with ample facilities including a 24-hour secretary service. But it is from the second to the thirteenth floor where the break-through in building technique is to be found; a series of prefabricated, single 'capsules' can be grafted on to the central

12 Assembly of the BC25 capsules

13 The Nakagin Business Hotel completed

14 Mori-Izumikyo Model
House: detail

15 Outside view

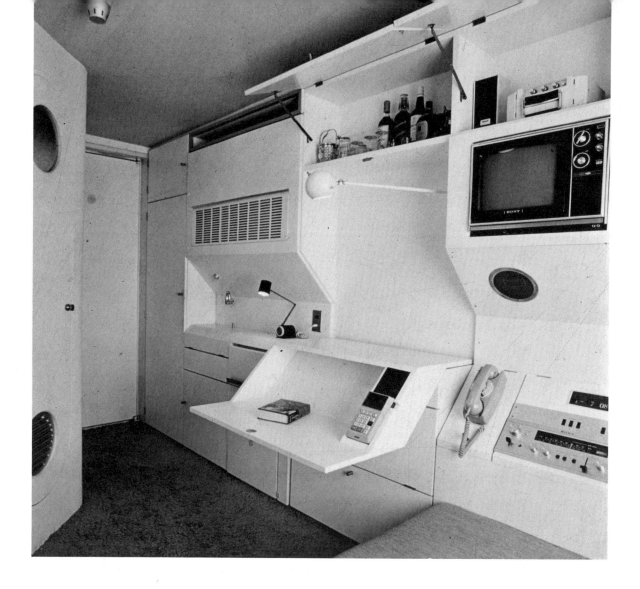

core in a countless number of ways. They consist of a lightweight steel frame structure with a 1·6mm-thick outer steel sheeting, protected by an undercoat of rust-preventive substance and spray-finished with Kenitex; the space available inside is 2·5m wide, 2·5m high and 4·0m deep (8'×8'×12'). In this particular building 140 capsules are located at each half-landing so that efficient use is made of vertical as well as horizontal space. Each capsule is provided with air conditioning unit and has facilities for the installation of air-cleaning devices, a small refrigerator and a sink. The furniture, from desk to bed to bath, is manufactured in specially designed integrated units. A 13" colour television set and a digital timer are part of standard equipment, but optional extras include a small electric desk calculator, amplifier, tape deck, speakers, and an automatic telephone answering device.

The remarkable versatility of this architectural 'cell' also permits its use in domestic architecture; thus a home can be extended according to need by the addition of extra capsules to the main structure, and the unobtrusive, clean lines of their design blend ideally with any landscape.

The Mori-Izumikyo Model House, the architect's own Summer house, is built on a slope in the holiday resort of Karuizawa. The main structure is of exposed concrete, on which four capsules are

attached to provide two bedrooms, one kitchen/dining room and a Tatami. The exterior of the capsules is sprayed a rich mahogany colour, the interior is finished with marble floors; Japanese cypress board covers the walls throughout the house. The essential simplicity and elegant proportion of the capsules lend themselves to a remarkable freedom and variety of decor, from the traditional Japanese Tatami to the Scandinavian-inspired dining room setting.

18 Living room

The Karuizawa Prince Hotel, Japan

Architect Kisho N Kurokawa

Set in the pine woods of the Karuizawa region, this resort hotel was planned in two main blocks: a rectangular building for the guest rooms and a pavilion-type structure containing the vast dining hall and lounge. Its striking appearance, with its graceful, gently curved copper-clad roof supported by massive columns, lends the whole place a distinctive quality of utter quiet and serene charm.

19 Karuizawa Prince Hotel: Outside view

20 Dining hall

The interior decoration makes abundant use of wood and is based on simple, strong lines. All guest rooms have picture windows looking across the woods to the mountains beyond, and the furniture is of 'shirodamo' wood and leather. A wide passage connects the guest rooms building with the pavilion; the wood used on floors and ceilings in the dining hall and in the lounge is pine, as if to echo the surrounding pine woods.

21 Lounge

22 Passage connecting the buildings

23 One of the guest rooms

The Marano Shoe Shop in Milano

Architect Sergio Asti
Photography by Mario Carrieri

In designing this shop the architect exploited to the full the long and narrow space available by defining it lengthways into three distinct sections, one outside and two within the shop.

The first section, illustrated below, consists of six mobile, triangular display cabinets which seem to lead the eye to the entrance door.

24 Open display

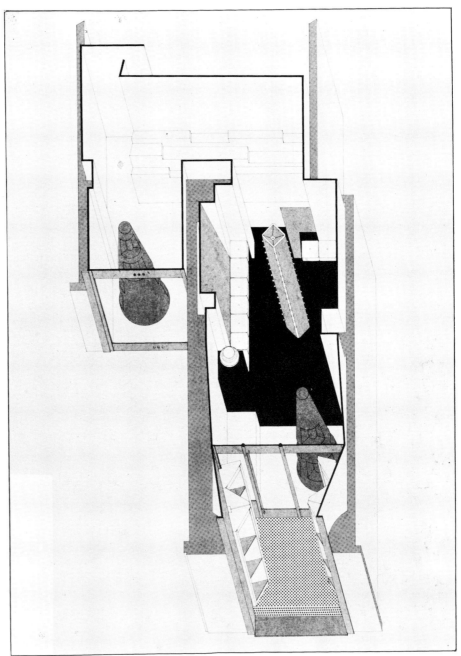

25 Plan

Once inside, a second display area focuses on a rotating conical module, and some steps lead to a larger fitting area. This space is separated from the rest of the shop by a compact arrangement of modules, by a long seat running along the walls, and by a truncated-pyramid shaped ceiling with a mirror set on its end. The freshness and lightness of the colour scheme and of the materials, the imaginative use of mirrors, and the neat, geometrical lines of walls and ceiling are the most interesting and exciting features of this shop.

26 Square central structure of
mirrors, with light fittings
on its edges

27 Fitting area with mirror set
at an angle and reflecting
the ceiling lined with
purposely made white and
lilac Abet Print laminate.
Seating of raw buckskin.
On the display module
stands 'Open Lotus', a lamp
designed and produced by
Venini

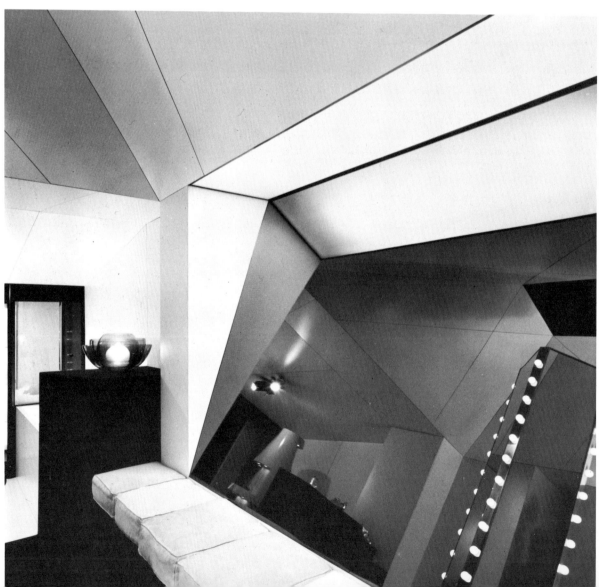

28 View from the back of the
shop: in the background
can be seen one of the
rotating yellow conic
modules used for display

The Young & Rubicam Advertising Agency, London

Architects Marcello Minale,
Brian Tattersfield,
Michele Provinciali
Photography by
Andrew Cockerell

The renovation of this office, occupying three floors of a converted late twenties factory on the Hampstead Road, was planned over a period of five years. Not surprisingly, the architects were briefed on the importance of a 'non-datable' interior and on the adoption of standard fittings wherever possible.

The present scheme is based on a terse, functional, unadorned simplicity of lines for the standard fittings and general decoration, which set off handsomely the occasional sculpture or the opulent materials such as leather and marble used for the more luxurious Conference and Dining rooms.

Its three floors are colour-coded green for the fourth floor, blue for the fifth and brown for the sixth floor. All ceilings are suspended, and splendid lighting effects are made possible by the installation of light fittings in the ceiling void (see opposite, Fig. 32). Plastic laminates are extensively used, such as Arborite for the white L-shaped units for secretaries and on the Dining room walls. Leather covers walls and table top in the Conference room. Seating is by Hille and Norrekilt. The dining table is one of Marcello Minale's designs and has a top of Napoleonic marble.

29 Fourth floor reception

31 Television theatre: detail of electronically operated sliding display panels

30 Television theatre: general view

32 Anteroom to television theatre

33 Sixth floor reception, the slatted suspended ceiling is painted brown on one side and white on the other, producing warm/cool light effect according to direction

34 view towards entrance;

35 One of the L-shaped units for secretaries

36 Corridor separating open typists' pool

37 Conference room; in the
background, display units
consisting of revolving
three-sided modules
electronically operated

38 Dining room

39

The Gerald Benny Showroom at Bear Lane, London

Architects
James Burford & Associates
Photography by Richard Einzig

After a prolonged search for suitable premises near the City, Gerald Benney decided to lease a site which is partly railway premises and partly in private ownership. Originally it belonged to a reputed London artesian well specialist, and subsequently became a scrap metal yard. When Mr Benney took the lease, its condition could only be described as horrifying.

Today as the visitor enters the building by the small, low entrance and lobby, the showroom expands as a tall, airy space with massive brick walls, where delicate, precious objects are displayed on black Jacobean oak chests. The effect is dramatic.

Daylight pours from overhead, with no other apertures to outside. Very rough brickwork of walls, piers and columns painted flat white, black steelwork, dark antique woods and the Berber carpet in natural wool colour all combine to create an enclosed, unexpectedly 'medieval' character to this space, and provide a powerful but unobtrusive background for silver and enamels.

39 Outside view

40 The old scrap metal yard

41 Same view, after conversion

left

42 Reception area; on the wall
black ceramic mural by
Paul Phipps

43 Display area with, in the
background, dining/kitchen
area

44 General view; the old forge
is now an open fireplace.
On the walls paintings and
prints by William Tucker and
Gordon Mouse

Villa on Lake Como, Italy

Architect and Interior Designer
Sergio Asti

Built on a steep slope on Lake Como, on three levels widening down to the water, this residence owes its character to the interplay of different architectural volumes alternating with open spaces. This plan allows for the numerous terraces to become closely related to the interior of the house and at the same time merge into lawns and grassy banks at various levels, so that the impression is one of living in total harmony with the surrounding landscape.

The entrance, at top level, leads immediately to the entertainment area. A spacious living/dining room, with sliding doors running along one entire wall, opens on to two large contiguous terraces overlooking the lake; the kitchen, scullery, shower room

45 General view across the water

46 The double terrace over the lake; on the left sliding doors to Living/Dining room

47 Upper Living room: dining area

and cloakroom are also included in this area. The middle level is devoted to family life; here too a small living/dining room opens on to a terrace, and the addition of a fireplace gives it a more intimate character. Here the provision of four bedrooms, two with breathtaking views over the lake, and of three bathrooms make a comfortable home of this house built on one of the most famous beauty spots of Italy; an alternative, not a complement to city dwelling. From the terrace adjoining the living room a staircase leads to the swimming pool and the boat-house below.

The interior decoration consists of a number of basic features adopted throughout. Black polished stone is used for the floors on the terraces and on the interior, with the exception of the bedrooms and of a raised area in the lower living room, fitted with honey-coloured, wall to wall carpet. Ochre-coloured plaster covers exterior and inside walls, again excepting the bedrooms where walls and ceilings are papered in white and brown checks, a pattern repeated on the velvet upholstery of the sofas in the living rooms. Everywhere else ceilings are of stucco painted a glossy shade of lobster pink. The wooden door fitments are painted silver. Most of the furniture, lighting and accessories were designed by Sergio Asti and produced industrially by Stilwood, Zanotta, Poltronova, Candle, Cedit and Salviati.

48 Lower Living room

49 Corner picture windows
from one of the bedrooms

50 One of the lower bedrooms

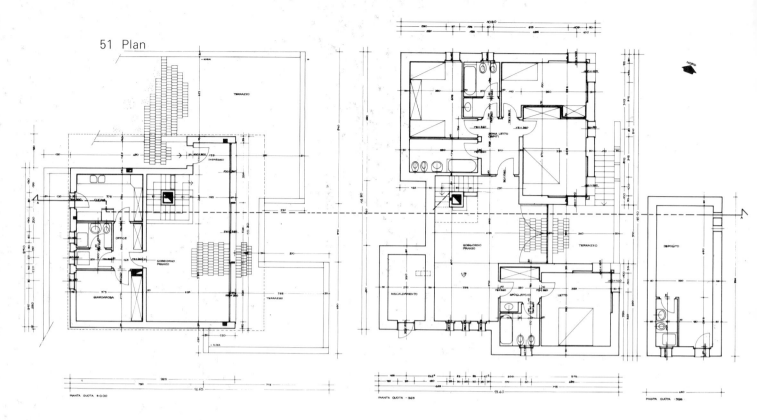

51 Plan

52 View over terrace and
garden levels from main
approach

53 Back entrance

Le Pavillon de Clavary, Southern France

Architect Tom Wilson
Photography by
Tim Street-Porter

The Pavillon de Clavary was built during the first half of the 19th century in the extensive grounds of the Château de Clavary. It started life as a coach house, but was changed to a garage with the advent of the motor car. When the architect decided to begin work on its conversion it contained 'decrepit 1920s cars, extinct electric generators, and agricultural machinery. The rooms upstairs still had traces of potatoes and corn which had been stored there.'

The outside, however, in its state of semi-decay, its rustic, naive façade vaguely reminiscent of Palladian architecture, had a certain appeal that the architect was determined to retain at all costs. Missing windows on the front were replaced with plate glass, without frames, so that even today, viewed at a distance, the house looks abandoned and half ruined. In contrast, every wall, floor and staircase of the interior was removed, the accommodation rearranged and the whole place transformed into a

55 Back view

54 View from the park

56 One of the front windows

57 Living room

58, 59 Living room

52

60 Kitchen

luxurious holiday home, though still possessing a homely, countrified character owing to the local traditional building materials employed in the decoration.

The whole ground floor became a living room. Masonry and plaster fireplace and side tables with rough marble tops were built and the floor was covered with local unglazed terracotta tiles arranged diagonally within nine rectangles. Select antique pieces and old masters seem to harmonize perfectly with the decor. Two huge sofas complete the furnishing.

The kitchen was added to the back of the house and has slate working surfaces on masonry supports, and old floor tiles bought from a demolition yard, The staircase and upper floor are paved with local 'navette' tiles, still being handmade as in the 18th century. The upper floor is occupied by four bedrooms and three bathrooms: Domed ceilings, glazed traditional tiles from Aubaigne and from the North of France are a distinctive feature. The bedrooms have fitted cupboards and are simply furnished.

61 Staircase to upper floor; detail showing the handmade 'navette' tiles, called after the design of a boat as drawn by a child

62 Bathroom lined with traditional yellow and brown Aubaigne tiles

54

63, 64 Master bedroom
suite; the bathroom is
lined with tiles from the
North of France

64

Family Holiday Home at Montorfano, Italy

Architect Ico Parisi
Photography by Giorgio Casali

Surrounded by beautiful woods, near Como, this holiday retreat was commissioned by its owner with the precise intent that it should become the meeting place for all the family, their children and friends, away from the constrictions of city life; a place where it would be possible 'to live together' in harmony with a natural environment.

The plan of the building is based on its gradual opening up on three sides towards the open countryside, from a cluster of three tiny bedrooms backing on to the woods to the three umbrella-shaped structures protecting the open-air living space.

The internal living area has dining/kitchen corner where stove adjoins dining table so that food preparation need not become a separate activity. A cylinder surmounted by a glass dome supplies natural and electric lighting and the mirrored table top, where the sky is reflected, increases the inside/outside relationship.

The furniture, designed by the architect, is of plastic laminates; sofas and beds are also upholstered in plastic. The floor is of ceramic tiles, walls and ceilings are painted. Dark grey, white and red form the colour scheme used throughout, inside and outside.

65 Outside view

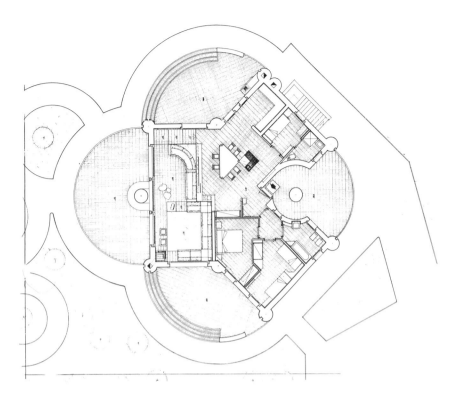

67 View of Family room from Living area. In the foreground two Perspex sculptures.

69 Dining area showing
multi-coloured square light
fittings, reflected on the
mirrored table

70 Dining/kitchen

Antidwelling Box, Japan

Architect Monta Mozuna
Photography by Shigeo Okamoto

Paradoxical as it might seem, this Antidwelling Box is to fulfil the needs of a contemporary dweller and his family!

The departure from traditional design originated from the architect's conviction that when planning a home, more often than not people get results opposite to those expected. This is mainly due to an architectural practice admitting in principle the adoption of duality of function, with parents/children, old/young users or communal/private, living/service requirements as determinant factors. By ignoring such preoccupations and basing the plan of a building on the designer's own concept there is a likelihood that the user will also benefit in the end.

The proposal illustrated consists of three cubes ('boxes') of reinforced concrete with a steel frame, one inside the other, connected by passages and stairs. Its striking appearance has an unexpected, perhaps unintended charm deriving from the uncompromising geometrical lines of its design. Viewed from the outside at night, the outer 'box' almost disappears from sight while the inner, brightly lit boxes appear to be floating in space.

The furniture is designed accordingly, with basic, simple lines enhanced by the use of contrasting colours, yellow and black for the wooden dining box, with blue walls, floors and ceiling. Storage facilities are offered by the stair-cupboard in the bedroom (Fig. 74). Light fittings are standard throughout.

71 General view

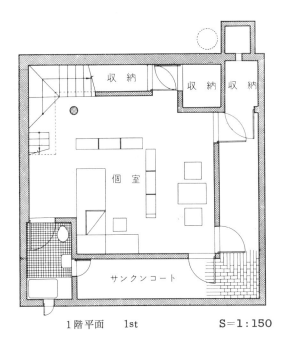

収納　収納収納

個室

サンクンコート

1階平面　1st　　　　　　S＝1：150

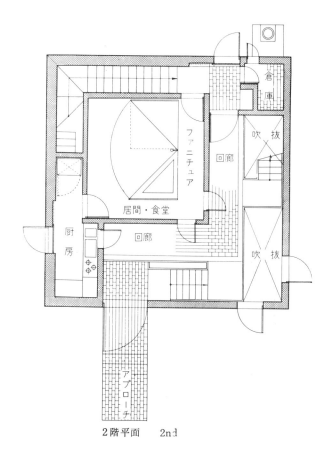

倉庫

ファニチュア

吹抜

回廊

居間・食堂

厨房

回廊

吹抜

アプローチ

2階平面　2nd

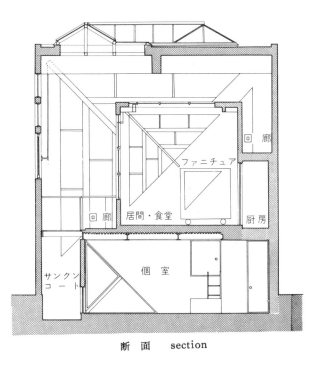

回廊

ファニチュア

居間・食堂

厨房

回廊

サンクンコート

個室

断面　section

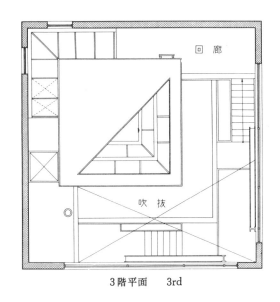

回廊

吹抜

3階平面　3rd

72 Plans

73 Outside view

74 Bedroom

75 Dining box closed

76 View across opened box
   to triangular window

77 Dining box opened

Opposite
78 Upward view from sunken
   court

The Stena Line Passenger Terminal at Göteborg

Architects Björn Westher,
Bengt Skog
Interior Designers
Stig H Sörensen, Hans Gerwins,
Hans-Agne Jakobsson

Conveniently situated near railway station and motorway, the new Masthuggs-Kai terminal serves all passenger traffic handled by Stena Line AB.

From its spacious Waiting Hall to Service Area and Restaurant and Cafeteria on the upper floor, the interior has a solid, distinguished elegance. The mahogany furniture, with comfortable, leather covered circular seating, is complemented by smart standard lights with shades of polished brass. Beech-sealed block floors, light blue aluminium ceiling and white rough plastered walls add an interesting and pleasant background.

The company's colours are used for coding: red indicates all communication, and is used for hand rails, lift and exit doors, information desks; white is for background surfaces and black for the counter tops.

The splendid light fittings have been specially designed by Hans-Agne Jakobsson.

79 General view of Göteborg Harbour

80 Outside view

81 View from the Waiting Hall

82 Restaurant and Cafeteria

83 Waiting Hall

84 Waiting Hall; detail of the chandelier

85 View from the Waiting Hall

Country Home at Goodleigh, England

Architects Aldington & Craig
Photography by Richard Einzig

Deeply set on a hillside site on the outskirts of a tiny village, the design of this house was inspired by the traditional Devon farm buildings which have slated roofs set low to the landscape or hugging the side of a hill or cliff.

Here the living room floor is level with the grass of the field outside and seems to be part of it. The whole of the tent-like roof plane, with the exception of that over the bedrooms, can be seen from the kitchen, living and dining areas and gives an impression of an even larger space. The main structure is of timber, with large areas of fixed glazing and glass doors opening on to the sloping garden; the gable ends are also completely glazed, and there is a thin clearstory glazing strip running the whole length of the building so that the roof appears to float above the walls.

The internal layout of the living accommodation produces a characteristic feeling of inside/outside relationship and increases the involvement with the landscape. Kitchen, living and dining areas are arranged around a tiny central open 'study', the only enclosure required by the brief, providing an area to confine the clutter of a desk without being cut off from the rest of the house.

88 *Opposite*
   Terrace view. In the foreground, pool with ornamental
   rocks and stone seat

86 Approach
87 Entrance Hall

The dining area, although basically part of the open plan, is under a very low flat ceiling and has an atmosphere of warmth and intimacy. The three bedrooms are enclosed in rectangles of brickwork. They have low ceilings above which there is loft storage space, but the diagonal pattern of the redwood wall boarding increases the feeling of height and asymmetry.

The materials used throughout are Lignacite block painted white and Swedish redwood board sealed with polyurethane varnish. Doors are flush and also white painted. Floors are golden brown quarry tiles for the open areas and carpet for the bedrooms.

90 Living area; detail

89 Kitchen/Dining; in the foreground, enclosed study area

91 Stairs from Living area to hall and bedrooms

92 Corridor leading to bedrooms

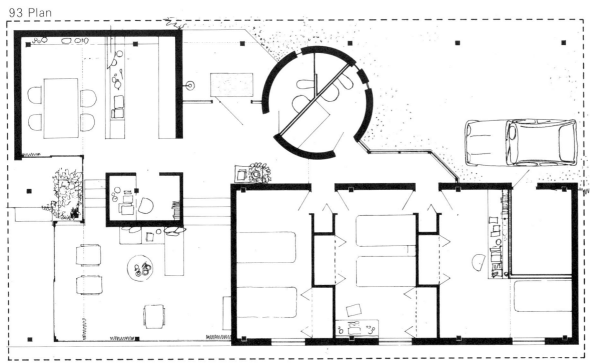

93 Plan

94 One of the bedrooms

Summer House on Patmos Island, Greece

Architect John Stefanidis
Photography by
Tim Street-Porter

There must come a moment in the life of a designer when he feels prepared to turn his back to all blandishments of modern 'comfort' rather than remove a single stone from buildings of such dignified and serene beauty as this tiny house on the island of Patmos. The architecture of this Cyclades village could be considered a masterpiece of urbanism; houses and streets are closely related and form a continuous, delicately balanced architectural whole. Unless changes are effected with great care and subtlety there is a danger of destroying the balance beyond repair.

96 View from street

95 Roof terrace view over Patmos

97 Detail of window in Living
   room; locally made crochet
   cushions are heaped on
   white quilted sofa

98 Living room

In this conversion, respect seems to have guided the work of the architect; the addition of two tiny bathrooms and of a stone staircase (replacing the original ladder) has been effected with the help and advice of local craftsmen who had received the tradition of this particular way of building from generations of past masons. Local men and women were also employed for the decoration, and the furniture designed by the architect is based on lattice work, an old local craft which is now enjoying a revival. For the furnishing the architect concentrated on the effect that light had on colours and textures, and oriental carpets, embroidery from Turkey and locally crocheted cushions blend ideally with brass objects and hand-painted pottery, in an atmosphere of unostentatious luxury.

99 Living room: detail showing a 1867 well from which water is still drawn

100 Old fireplace has been converted into a shelved alcove in the kitchen; the ceiling is made of bamboo canes tightly packed between wooden beams

101 Bedroom; locally made
latticed furniture stained
pale blue

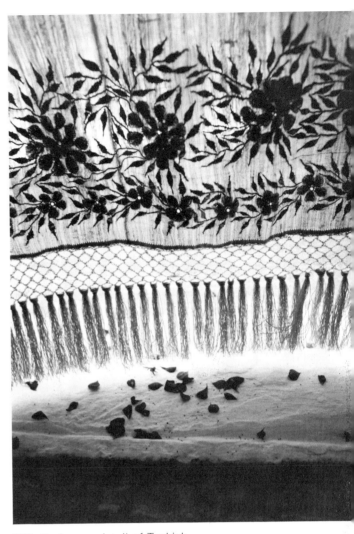

102 Bedroom; detail of Turkish
curtain, embroidered and
fringed in silver

103 Bedroom; general view

A Special Care Unit in London

Architects Foster Associates
Photography by
Tim Street-Porter

Flexibility was the keynote in the planning of this special care unit, at a time when change was foreseen in the schooling methods for the severely handicapped child.

The architects opted for a fixed central service core, flanked on both sides by two flexible areas defined by movable partitions and sliding screens. The central core is occupied by WC/changing and laundry facilities; it is fully glazed for efficient staff supervision and to allow the children to observe the activity area, thus relieving some of the unpleasant aspects of incontinence. Above the service area is a plant room housing heating and air-conditioning installations, with ducts hidden above the suspended ceiling throughout the building. Heating is radiated through the ceiling.

Great care has been taken to make the unit as inviting and reassuring as possible by a bold use of positive colours: orange for the wall to wall nylon carpet in the activity area, yellow and pink for the movable partitions and sliding screens, green for the sanitary fittings. The outside court is enclosed by a palisade of asbestos panels painted with swooping stripes of blue and yellow overflowing on the tarmac ground. A wide range of imaginative play equipment includes mobiles and special plastic inflatables designed at the Royal College of Art.

104 General view of play court

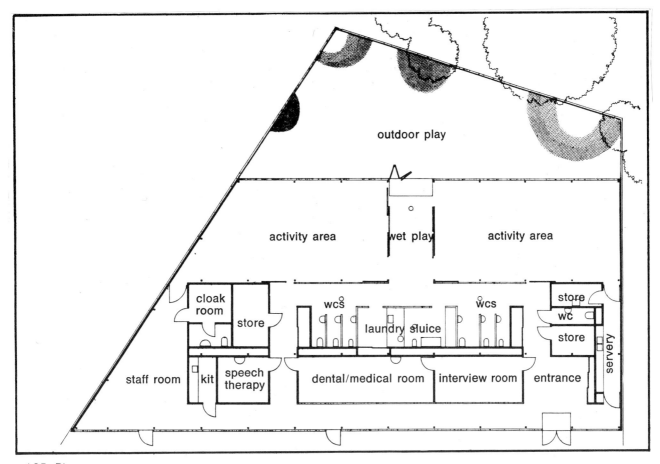

outdoor play

activity area   wet play   activity area

cloak room

store

wcs   wcs

store

wc

store

servery

staff room   kit   speech therapy

laundry sluice

dental/medical room   interview room   entrance

105 Plans

106 View from indoor activity area

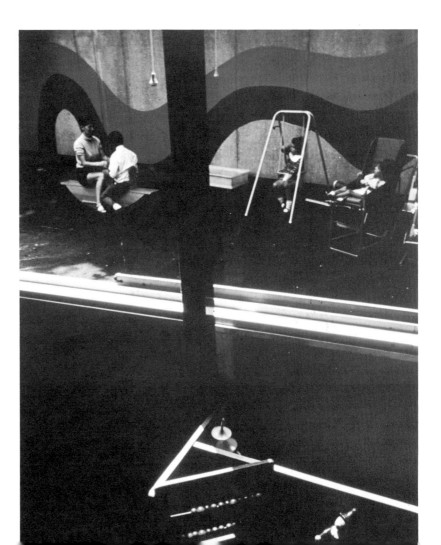

107, 108 Indoor activity
and specially designed play
equipment

108

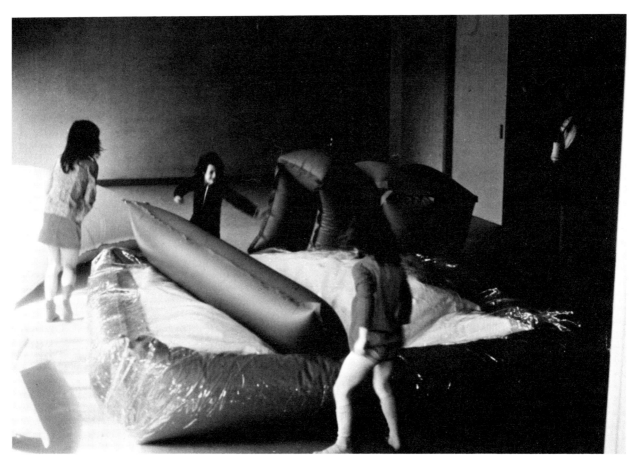

109 Children at play on
inflatable plastic equipment

110 Service area

A Mews Conversion in South Kensington, London

Architects Anne and Christopher Moorey
Photography by George Tanner of John Maltby Ltd

Two garages-cum-flat near Hyde Park (originally stables and lodgings) were converted for a professional couple weary of daily commuting from outer suburbs to city.

One of the garages was to be retained in use; the remaining building had to provide a compact living unit suitable for entertaining and furnished with a small collection of antiques.

The architects re-designed the stairs by returning and extending the first eight treads into an open railed half landing. This solution bars direct access from street level to the upper floor and defines clearly a small 'lobby' which leads on to the living/dining area, formerly the larger of the two garages, through an arched opening to the right of the entrance door. A second opening allows the reception area to flow from main entrance to kitchen door to the foot of the stairs. A counter separates dining from kitchen, and the whole room receives light from the large

111 Outside view

GROUND FLOOR PLAN   FIRST FLOOR PLAN

STORE

GALLEY
KITCHEN

COUNTER.

2ND BEDROOM/STUDY

8700 mm

LANDING

UP

DINING AREA

DOWN

GARAGE

BEDROOM

LIVING ROOM.

GLAZED

RAISED
AREA

112 Plan

ENTRANCE

7400 mm

113 Kitchen/Breakfast area

114 View from main entrance

115 Dining area

116 Bedroom

window which has replaced the old garage doors. The design of the antiqué dining table suggested the arched line of the suspended ceiling over the counter, and walls and ceiling are finished with white stipple plaster to enhance the patina of the old woods. The floor is maple strip throughout.

The upper floor was entirely rearranged: the main bedroom has a glazed panel in one wall to provide light for the stairs. A study/second bedroom was created from the existing kitchen and, like the bathroom, is lit by overhead skylights.

The whole upper floor is covered by carpet.

A Designer's Home and Studio, London

Designers Barbara Brown,
Ron Nixon
Photography by Sam Sawdon

An Edwardian house in South East London was bought by textiles designers Barbara Brown and Ron Nixon to become their home and studio.

No alterations were made to the existing layout, apart from demolishing half the wall between kitchen and dining room. Now pine boards line the dining area, and at the same time conceal the central heating pipes. The studio is also a living room where friends are entertained, and one of the three bedrooms is used as a workshop, its space taken up almost entirely by a huge loom where the beautiful wool hangings are made. Cork tiles cover floors and line the whole bathroom ('the cosiest place in the whole house!').

The furniture, with only one exception, was bought second hand or at the sales; surplus stores and junk shops were conscientiously raided to provide the accessories, one of the 'finds'

117 Dining area
118 Kitchen area

88

119, 120 Bathroom

being the handsome light shade over the dining table. The superficial observer may be led to wonder how such high standards could be reached without the help of a qualified interior designer and a small team of specialized craftsmen. Perhaps the answer is a simple one: two artists, untrained in building techniques, wanted very much a place of their own for living and working. Being very gifted artists, and valuing most of all their work and their own way of life, they naturally and directly express these values in whatever activity they happen to be engaged. Food for thought in this consumer-orientated society of ours!

121 Bedroom

123 Studio; on table and wall,
hangings designed and
made by Barbara Brown
and Ron Nixon

A Conversion in South Eaton Place, London

Architect Zeev Aram &
Associates
Photography by Sam Sawdon

A late Georgian terraced house had, before renovation and conversion, two or three rooms on each of its four narrow floors, dark passages and a confined and claustrophobic atmosphere. The architects rearranged the internal layout, with the exception of the top floor, to suit the needs of a family with two children and an au pair.

125 Ground floor plan

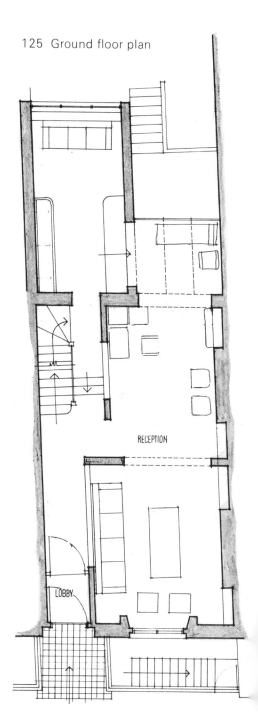

124 Detail of reception area showing one of the openings cut into the inner wall

126 Living room

127 Studio with audio-visual
equipment
128 View to glazed living room
extension from studio

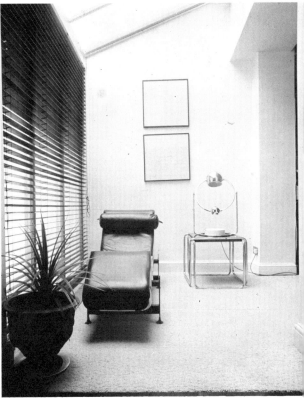

The basement contains now a kitchen and family dining area and a service area, where laundry, central heating and central vacuum cleaning unit are efficiently grouped.

The ground floor is taken by a reception and living area, mainly for use by the parents. The dividing wall between the two original reception rooms was removed and large openings were cut into the inner wall, so that the living room now appears to extend to the full width of the house (Figs. 124, 126). The rear wall was extended 6' to provide a link with the study, which is also marked by a drop in floor level (Fig. 127). A floor to ceiling glazed area occupies most of the rear wall in the living room and study and looks on to the paved garden.

The flat roof over the study, covered by Italian tiles, has become a small patio reached from a half-landing, where a cupboard and worktop provide a mini-office for the lady of the house. The first floor is occupied by a master bedroom suite and the top floor has two bedrooms and a bathroom.

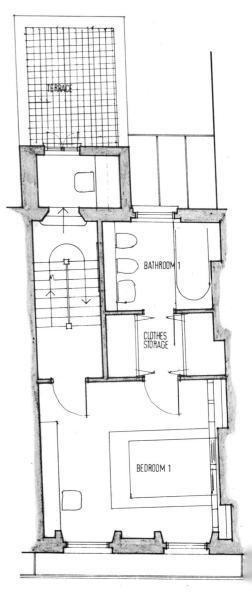

129 First floor plan

130 View of roof-garden

131, 132 Master bedroom;
the bed, designed by Zeev
Aram & Associates, is on a
raised timber frame and
houses storage and
concealed lighting

Reception area, stairs and first floor are unified by a heavy-textured oatmeal wool carpet and all walls are painted white. This neutral colour scheme gives an impression of space and of calm, luminous airiness. It provides an ideal background to the owners' collection of beautiful modern furniture, prints and paintings.

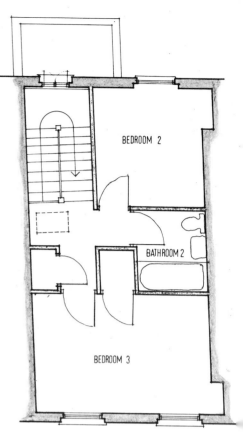

Second floor plan

133 Staircase to second floor

134 Nursery

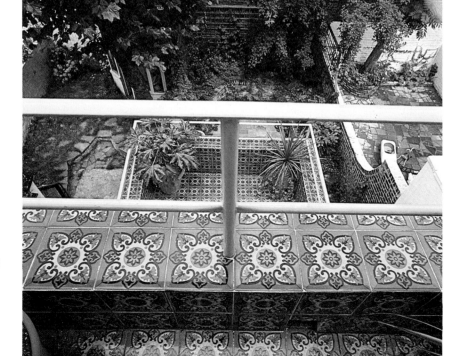

135 View of roof garden from
balcony on second floor

The Home of the Architect, St. Louis, California

Architect Gyo Obata
Photography by
Hedrich-Blessing and
George Cserna

Nature lavished unplanned landscaping on the architect's own home in a St Louis suburb, but Gyo Obata himself, Design Partner of Hellmuth, Obata & Kassabaum, provided the water view by filling up an abandoned quarry pit (overpage). Woods and meadow were retained in their natural state and make the secluded site seem much larger than the three acres it occupies.

The house has five levels, all of which are opened to the little lake by large areas of glass, some of them extended by decks or porches (below).

98

The upper floor, entered from a parking space behind the house, has a storey-and-a-half living room, whose ceiling slopes down beside the fireplace into a contemporary version of the old-fashioned inglenook (page 101). Above is a gallery/studio. Up half a level from the living room are four bedrooms and two bathrooms. Down half a level are dining room (Fig. 139), kitchen/ breakfast room, and down another half level, under the living room, are a large family room and the utility room. The whole house is airy and open because it was built following the slope from parking lot to lake. The sturdy timber framing is simple and exposed.

139 Dining room

140 Detail of inglenook
fireplace

141 View of living room from
gallery

Architect Clyde Rich
Photography by
Tim Street-Porter
Louis Reens
*Photos No. 143, 144, 146, 147,
150 by courtesy of*
House & Garden Guides

An Apartment on Central Park West New York

142   The living room from the
conversation pit; in the
foreground Rudi Stern's
mirrored boxes filled with
neon sculptures and
covered by plate glass are
part of the unit.

An apartment on Central Park West, New York, was rearranged and decorated for a television film producer and his wife, mainly for work and entertaining. A particularly sensitive scheme, based on reflecting surfaces and bold use of colour, defines areas dedicated to entertainment or study, and the owners' extensive collection of modern art pieces is integrated and sometimes incorporated in the furnishing (see Fig. 142 opposite). The entrance hall (Fig. 143) has a green-stained wooden floor which is repeated throughout the living and dining rooms, thus unifying the reception/entertainment area. Mirrored walls reflect the violet glossy painted ceiling and wood trim, and two handsome chain stitch rugs are illuminated by overhead projectors.

143   Entrance hall; the
illuminated plastic
sculpture on left foreground
is by Gary Strutin, who also
made the low round table
designed by Clyde Rich
(right). The two 'bicycle'
chairs are by Veli Majo.

145 Living room; the
conversation pit seen from
the entrance

A former dark closet off the entrance hall was transformed into an elegant bar (Fig. 144) with silver and violet wallpaper, violet painted wood trim and cabinets, glass shelves, mirrors, recessed lighting. Guatemalan belts hanging on left door add an exotic note to the sophisticated decor.

Subtle shades of green contribute to a mood of serenity and playfulness in the living room (Figs. 145–148). The furniture is low in a lofty, airy space, with a few round shapes adding humour and wit to a design which relies almost exclusively on square, functional lines.

At the window end (Fig. 145) one side wall and the ceiling are entirely faced with mirrors; a raised conversation 'pit' of green Formica is multiplied and given visual depth by infinite reflections and illusions of distance. Heavy cotton upholstery, dyed green to match, covers the latex foam seating and offers a delightful background to the rich silk, velvet, metallic and Indian fabrics of the numerous cushions in this area. A fibreglass sculpture by Richard Kalina, neon sculptures by Rudi Stern and a 'Spring Painting' by Joan Snyder (see Fig. 142) are among the works of art in this room.

Above the Joan Snyder painting two speakers controlled by the central hi-fi installations in the library provide musical entertainment. Light emanates from a Plexiglas game table by Clyde Rich and Gary Strutin; the four chairs are by Joe Colombo (Fig. 147). Just in front of the conversation pit, a glass and stainless steel coffee table rests on a white Greek flokati rug and is complemented by two green fibreglass 'Gyro' chairs by Eero Aarnio (Fig. 146).

146, 147 Details of living room

148 Living room; detail

149 Dining room

The dining room (Fig. 149) has walls and ceiling painted sky blue, a wall painting by Allan d'Arcangelo, cabinet work by Clyde Rich, and furniture designed with maximum flexibility in mind. The dining table consists of four equal squares of plastic laminate in an off-white colour, with polished chrome pedestals; they can be separated to accommodate up to sixteen people. Under a yellow sculpture, a buffet glides on castors to reveal marble block, wooden block and warming surface insets so that the master of the house, a dedicated gourmet cook, can make last minute food preparations for his guests. Eight vinyl upholstered Breuer chairs complete the furnishing.

By contrast, the library (Fig. 150) is dark and soft, in vibrant colours picked up from the fabric which covers the sofa and lines the vertical blinds at the window end; red-violet for walls and ceiling, blue-violet for trim and book-cases (not shown). Carpeting, designed by David Hicks, is in the two shades plus white. The oval graphic on the far wall, by Tina Matkovic, doubles as a screen for the projecting room opposite. The desk is of rosewood, and the chair with matching ottoman is covered with black leather.

150 Library

151, 152, 153 Sam Herman working at the Royal College of Art, London

Modern glass Review

Foreword by Otto Wittman and Robert F Phillips

Brilliant, brittle, fragile, fluid in form, glass has been a rare commodity and highly prized throughout most of history. It is only within the last hundred years when it has been possible to make glass by machine that it has become a common and inexpensive substance. In antiquity it was more rare than gold, and as precious as the finest jewels.

No other material can duplicate the optical richness of glass; its qualities include endless possibilities of colour, reflection, translucency, and transparency.

Glass is among the very few apparently solid substances which have no crystalline structure, and has for this reason often been described as a 'super-cooled liquid' — a substance that has passed from a molten to a rigid state without structural change.

Glass is unique among the materials available to artists in that it must be worked at a temperature too hot to handle. Unlike any other artist, the glassworker must keep his work at arm's length as he shapes the molten material. While glass has been made by man for almost 4000 years, the most revolutionary event in the history of glassworking was the introduction of the blow pipe which historians generally agree occurred shortly before the birth of Christ. The methods and ingredients used to make glass and the tools used to form it have changed little over the centuries, with the exception of the ingenious machines which brought about mass production in the 20th century. These were however only the first of a number of new means made available to the glassworker by the development of industry and technology. Not only have contemporary craftsmen further refined traditional disciplined off-hand glass blowing techniques, but they have also applied other forming methods utilising industrially produced material, such as sagging and bending sheets and blocks of semi-molten glass and casting molten glass in metal moulds. In addition to fuming, a technique using chemicals to impart a changing iridescence to the surface colour, a number of other surface treatments are employed. They range from sandblasting and engraving which cut into the surface, to electroplating and painting which coat it.

A new interest in glass has arisen during the last decades; artists from other fields, particularly sculptors, architects and ceramicists, are attracted to actual glassblowing by the endless possibilities of this very ancient material, adding a further dimension to the establishment of glass as an art form.

Otto Wittmann, Director, The Toledo Museum of Art
Robert F Phillips, Curator of Contemporary Art, The Toledo Museum of Art
Paul Smith, Director, The Museum of Contemporary Crafts

International Glass
by Michael Robinson

The impact of Japanese art and of early Chinese art during the late 19th century and the beginning of the 20th influenced deeply our approach to the materials we use. The idea that all substances have natures of their own and that the seemingly lowliest among them can become tremendous mediums when properly understood is now part of our own awareness, and as their value and possibilities are appreciated the distinctions held for so long between artists and craftsmen, arbitrarily based on choice of medium, become blurred and eventually break down. A new role emerges and rapidly becomes one key figure in contemporary art history: the designer.

At the beginning of the 20th century, many artists, attracted by the possibilities offered by familiar but re-discovered mediums, gave a new direction to their aims and objectives. Their initial explorations, discoveries, failures and successes, formed the basis of the schools and training centres for designers which today provide a thorough, professional training in a given medium and impart a healthy respect for the characteristics of others. As a result, traditions and techniques became known internationally. Czechoslovakia, one of the first countries to establish schools in glass design, concentrated on cutting and engraving, whilst Italy followed the Venetian tradition of blowing and furnace manipulation. These national characteristics can still be traced but are less and less obvious as designers tend to become more cosmopolitan. International exhibitions and publications facilitate the communication of ideas, techniques and styles amongst artist craftsmen, and personal responses and associations tend to be more influential than traditional styles. Although most factories employ a residential designer many welcome the stimulus of a different outlook and hire or commission the work of reputable international glass artists.

The importance of the designer centres on his personal involvement with the method of production, be it a team of colleagues, craftsmen or an industrial machine. This combination of one man's vision and another's skill is the mainspring for the

110

production of better designed, more attractive glass objects. In the recent past, the work of such teams as the Galle and Tiffany Studios, Orrefors and its designers, and of contemporary artists such as Pavel Hlava, is evidence of the viability of the synchronised group, each of its members contributing his own skill under the direction of the master designer. Many works of art are being created in glass houses throughout the world through this beautifully sensitive association of talents. However, this is only the tiny inspiring tip of the iceberg of glass production; each piece produced is an artistic endeavour demanding the close attention of designer and team at every stage. More often factory teams work to measured drawings and specifications without the personal direction of the designer. Good glass can still be produced by this method, providing the designer is familiar with his craftsmen and does not attempt to be too ambitious, but the danger of misinterpretation is always present and if the designer loses contact with the team he could be directing nothing better than a human conveyor belt.

Such danger does not threaten the designer working with mechanised techniques; the machine cannot suffer from lack of verbal communication! It can repeat endlessly simple or complex movements and reproduce flawlessly the task it has been programmed to perform. If the designer is aware of the particular nature of machine-made glass there is no reason why he should not produce objects as attractive and significant as those made by hand. The frequent tirades made against the lack of character and oppressive sameness of inexpensive, badly designed, mass-produced glass can undoubtedly be appreciated but it is unfair to brand in this manner all machine made production, especially when so much of the more expensive, so called 'hand-made' glass offered as an alternative is equally characterless and shoddy. The beauty of an object lies in itself, and the machine when properly used can produce aesthetically satisfying objects just as well as the craftsman can become an insensitive cog in a profit oriented machine.

The designer-craftsman combination has been the most powerful force during most of this century, but it is quite likely that a new figure will have taken the helm towards its end: the glass artist. Working alone at the furnace, and governed by a more selective relationship to his medium, the individual glass-worker is becoming more and more a leading influence and inspiration, and is probably the most significant contribution that our century will make to glass history.

The well organized Czechoslovakian glass industry with its training schools sited in glass-making areas has for long provided the student with the chance to blow his own pieces, and much of the superb Czech glass is produced not only by designer-blower teams but also by glass artists working alone. However, the real breakthrough occurred in the early 1960s, with the invention of small, cheap and easily built furnaces, and of a glass formula that would melt at relatively low temperatures. Harvey Littleton and Dominick Labino, the two American innovators who devised this revolutionary formula, have played a very important role in studio glass. Their work and their teaching attracted a number of talented younger artists and soon the movement they initiated spread across the Atlantic. A former sculptor and pupil of Harvey Littleton, Sam Herman, came to England as a Fulbright Scholar in the late 1960s and first introduced the new technique to this country. In 1969 an exhibition of his work at the Crafts Centre of Great Britain was so successful that a new idea originated: the setting up of a small studio where facilities for glassblowing could be hired and where members of the public could watch glassblowing, sharing in some way the experience of creative work. Sam Herman was the most active force in this project, and today The Glasshouse has become a well known centre where glassblowing is taught, studio glass produced, exhibited and sold, and where artists meet people interested in their work.

In conclusion, we can observe three main lines along which the development of studio glass will probably follow its course: the small domestic production furnace, where utilitarian objects are made much on the same scale as the studio pottery; the artist-designer, making and decorating glass still within its traditional concepts, whose work has affinities with that of the designer-craftsman team and yet displays more of the personal struggle; finally, the artist working in a variety of mediums who uses glass as a vehicle for a particular aim, and even employs it in conjunction with other materials. This last figure, strongly linked with his environment, makes the most revolutionary use of glass; he provokes the greatest reaction and, stepping beyond the known and accepted traditions, is doing most to expand the meaning, application and value of glass.

Michael Robinson, Assistant Keeper of Art, The Ulster Museum

American Glass Today
by Otto Wittmann

A dramatic change in the role of the individual glassworker has come about within the past twelve years in the United States. In contrast to the earlier 20th century commercial method in both the United States and Europe where art glass was produced by craftsmen who formed shapes in three dimensions which had been designed on paper by an artist, a new concept has developed in which the designer and craftsman are one and the same.

The concept of a designer who is also a craftsman is not new. A general revival of interest in studio craftsmanship began in the United States in the 1930s. While there has been great interest and development in the craft concept in ceramics, textiles and metal, there was no parallel interest in the craft of glassworking until the late 1950s, when designer-craftsmen in the field of ceramics felt that the medium of glass also had great potential for creative expressive forms. Only the technical ability to work the material was lacking.

In 1962 a workshop for the actual production of studio glass took place for the first time in Toledo, when in March of that year the Toledo Museum of Art invited Harvey Littleton, then an instructor in ceramics at the University of Wisconsin who was also actively interested in studio glass, to conduct a seminar in glassblowing. This first creative glass workshop, held in a small garage on the Toledo Museum's grounds, had its moments of excitement, frustration and hilarity. A small furnace was constructed by Littleton and eight students, most of whom were experienced potters interested in the possibility of using glass as a new medium. The furnace would not develop heat sufficient to melt the glass formula first devised. It was then that Dominick Labino, at that time research vice-president for Johns-Manville Fiber Glass Corporation, and an avocational student in several Museum art classes, was invited to solve the technical difficulties encountered. With the use of a new formula Labino provided the seminar with molten glass. However, attempts to blow forms from the molten material were only exploratory. Through the advice of Harvey Leafgreen, retired 69-year-old Libbey Glass Company glassblower, the group learned almost forgotten methods.

A second Toledo Museum seminar in June 1962, again under the direction of Littleton with twelve different students and a newly built furnace, expanded the knowledge and possibilities of glass craftsmanship. Labino, who had provided the original formula for the first seminar, had been so stimulated by the possibilities that by June he had established his own private workshop on his farm in Grand Rapids, Ohio. He retired from his company in 1965, and today devotes much of his time to glassworking and scientific research. Littleton returned to the University of Wisconsin where he has continued to work and teach ever since. He not only set up his own glass workshop at home, but developed courses in glass-working at the University from which emerged many of the glass craftsmen who are the leaders in their field.

Today, glassworking in taught in more than 50 universities, colleges and art schools across the country and is practised by artist-craftsmen in all parts of our country as well as in parts of Europe. The Museum of Contemporary Crafts gave early recognition to some of the leading glassworkers through one-man exhibitions as early as 1964, and the Toledo Museum of Art organized biennial National exhibitions since 1966 which have received nationwide circulation by the Smithsonian Institution to many other museums. The most recent, *American Glass Now*, included the work not only of some of the founders of this movement, but also the innovative and advanced work of a 'second generation'.

During the past decade the metamorphosis of glassworking from a craft to an art occurred in the United States. The artists working in glass today are searching for new forms, combining glass with other materials, and developing new techniques independent of industrial technology. They are exploring new horizons as part of the mainstream of contemporary art.

Otto Wittmann, Director, The Toledo Museum of Art

Opposite

156
Drinking set, clear crystal
Designed by F Meydam for
Royal Leerdam, Holland

157
'A 200' series of drinking
glasses, clear crystal
Designed by Hans R Janssen
for Gral-Glashütte GmbH,
West Germany

158
'RH 478/7' candle holders,
clear crystal; 8 and 11 (3$\frac{1}{4}$"
and 4$\frac{3}{8}$") high
Designed by Hans R Janssen
for Glashütte Leichlingen
GmbH, West Germany

154
'Shizuku Glass' mould blown
vases; blue/smoke or green/
smoke 14 ×9 (5$\frac{1}{2}$" ×3$\frac{1}{2}$")
Designed and made by
Masakichi Awashima, Japan

155
'Gaissa' hand-blown tumblers,
clear glass; five sizes
Designed by Tapio Wirkkala for
Iittala Glassworks, Finland

156

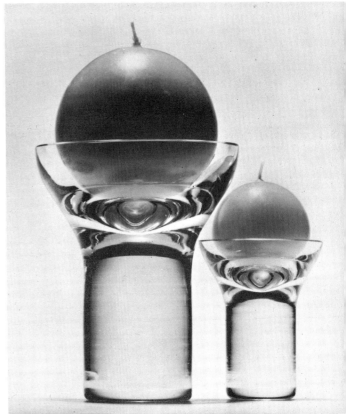

158

157

159

161

159, 160
Sculptured bowl No 4267/121,
clear crystal; about 15 (6") high
Hurricane lamp No 2371/101,
clear crystal; about 35 (13¾")
high
Both designed by Olle Alberius
for Orrefors, Sweden

161
'Ballonglas' hand made clear
glasses; 14·6, 11·9, 9 (5¾",
4¾", 3½")
Designed by Per Lütken for
Holmegaard of Copenhagen,
Denmark

162
'Gianmaria', three hand-blown
crystal bottles grouped on a
silver stand
Designed by Carla Venósta for
Bacci, Italy

163
Candelabrum for Emmaboda
Church, glass and wrought iron,
2 m×1·5 m (6' 6¾"×4' 11")
Designed by Erik Höglund and
made at Boda Glasbruk,
Sweden

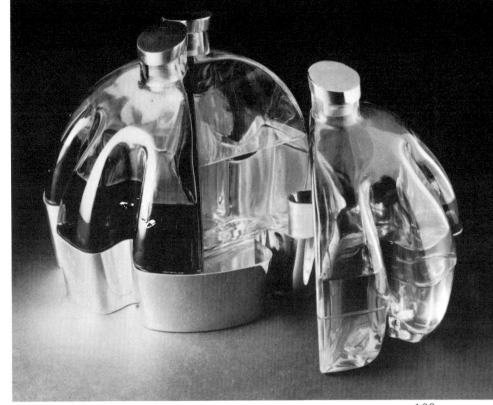

162

163

164
'Lace' bowls and containers,
opal and clear glass
Designed by Owe Thorssen and
Birgita Carlsson for Venini, Italy

165 Glass bowl from a series
of six
Designed by Sigurd Persson
for Kosta Glasbruk, Sweden

166
Bottle sculpture, hand blown,
with flame puncture decoration;
20 (8") high
Designed by Pavel Hlava and
made at the Včelnïcka Works,
Cesky Křyšťál np, Czechoslovakia

165

166

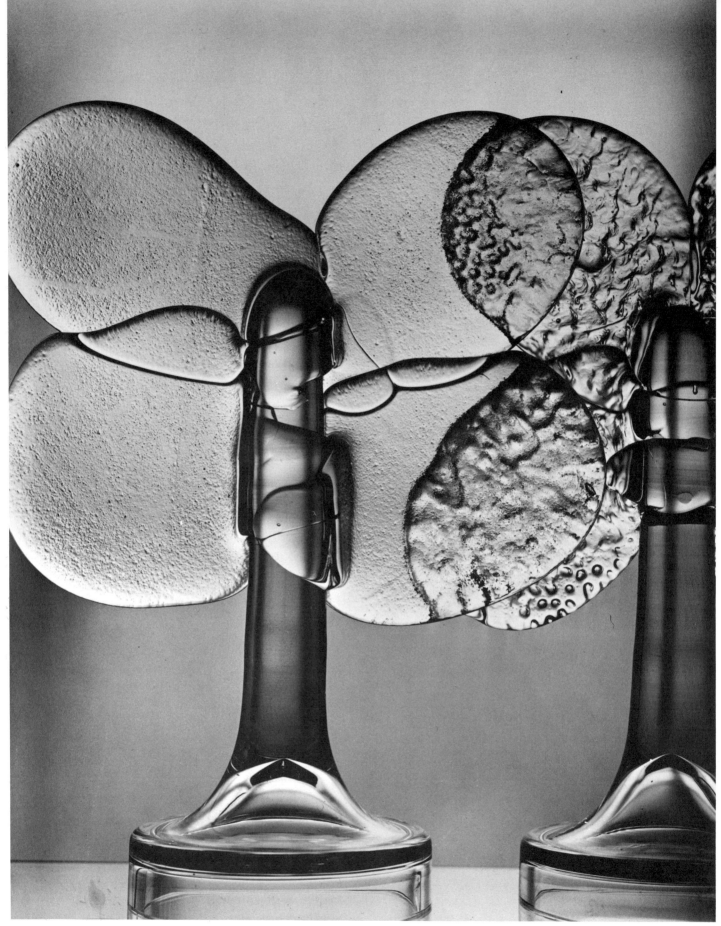

167
'Perhonen' (Butterfly),
sculpture of moulded crystal
on cast iron; 30×25 (11¾″×9¾″)
Designed by Nanny Still for
Riihimäen Lasi Oy, Finland

168
'Hockus Pockus' candle holder
or eggcup, clear pressed
crystal; 5×5 (2″×2″)
Designed by Nanny Still for
Riihimäen Lasy Oy, Finland

169
'Demodé', series of flower
holders of various sizes and
colours; the molten, multi-
coloured glass paste is forced
into a special mould by
compressed air; the resulting
pattern is purely accidental
Designed by Sergio Asti for
Venini, Italy

168

169

170

170
Decorative bottles, hand blown
Designed and made by
Masakichi Awashima, Japan

171
'Dawn' glass sculpture; detail,
40 (15¾") high
Designed by Oiva Toikka and
made at Oy Wärtsilä Ab,
Finland

172
Glass sculpture, clear and green
crystal with air bubbles
decoration; 18·5 (7¼") high
Designed by Wärff for Kosta
Boda Glasbruk, Sweden

171

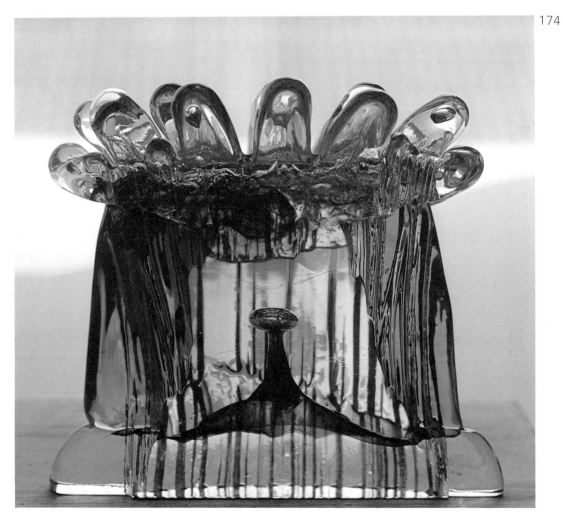

173
Unique piece, open mould
blown and free blown, clear
glass with red and blue cave;
40·5×25·5 (16"×10")
Designed by Marvin B Lipofsky
and made by master blower
Gianni Toso at Venini glassworks, Italy

174
'Landscape' sculpture;
22 (8¾") high
Designed and made by Ann
Wärff, at Kosta Glasbruk,
Sweden

175
'Circus Teapot', free blown
multicoloured glass, 'Murrina'
technique; 20·5 (8") high
Designed and made by Richard
Marquis, California

175

176
'Railo' bottles, hand-blown in metal mould, clear glass with red glass stopper; 20 and 30 (8" and 12" high) high
Designed by Nanny Still for Riihimäen Lasi Oy, Finland

177
Sculpture with flame puncture decoration; two separate hemispheres are fused together
Designed and made by Pavel Hlava at the Ceský Křišťál np, Czechoslovakia

178
From the 'Leerdam Glass-vormcentrum Color Series 1970', Green and Yellow unique piece, blown in three parts to fit together, cut and polished; 35·5×61 (14"×24")
Designed by Marvin B Lipofsky and made by master blower Van der Linden, at Royal Leerdam, Holland

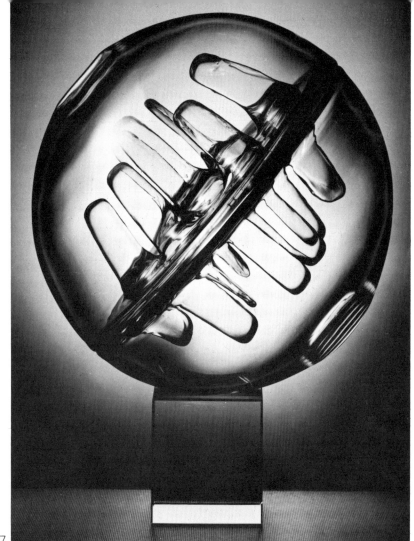

177

178

179
'Blue Sculpture', mould and
free blown
Designed and made by Kabey
Ashi, Japan

180
Plate, crystal glass with silver
chloride decoration; 35·5 (14")
diameter
Designed and made by Jane
Gilchrist at the Royal College
of Art, London

181
Plate; 91·5 (36") diameter
Designed and made by Sam
Herman at the Royal College of
Art, London

180

181

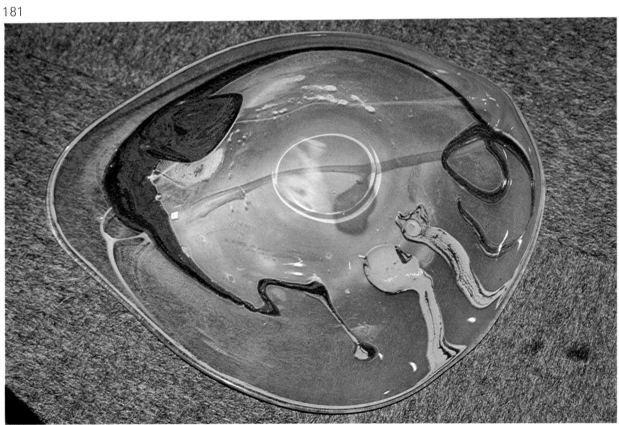

182

182
'Earth Globe', sand blasted
glass, clear, blue, green, amber;
45 (17¾") diameter
Designed by Wärff and made at
Ab Åforsgruppen, Sweden

183
'Stoppered Decanter with Bike',
free blown clear glass; 40·5
(16") high
Designed and made by William
Bernstein, USA

184
Bowl, clear crystal, cut,
engraved and sand blasted;
Designed and made by
Peter Dreiser, England

183

184

185
'Crystal Object'; 15 (6")
diameter;
Designed by F Meydam and
made at Royal Leerdam,
Holland

186
Containers, various sizes
Designed by Flavio Barbini and
made for Barbini, Italy

185

186

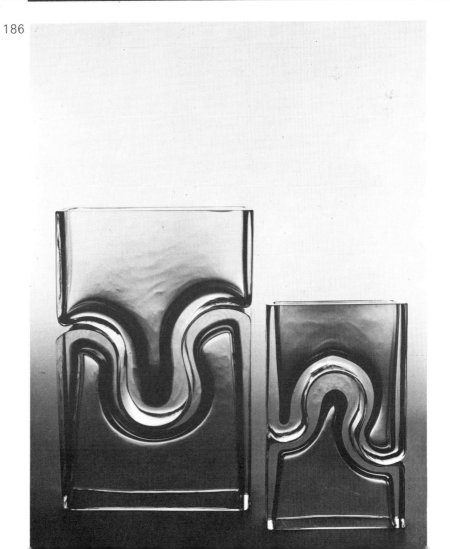

187
'Hand form' off-hand blown,
hot tooled, with trailed pattern;
Designed and made by Joel
Philip Myers, USA

188
Plate, acid etching with pressed
motif, brown on grey background; 45 (17¾″) diameter
Designed by Raoul Goldoni
for Barbini, Italy

187

188

189
Sculpture, hand blown, silvered
green glass; 30·5 × 30·5 × 15·2
(12″ × 12″ × 6″)
Designed and made by Sam J
Herman at the Royal College of
Art, London

190
'Three Forms', white irradiated
crystal;
Designed by Raoul Goldoni for
Livio Seguso, Italy

189

190

191
'Untitled', free blown crystal,
with multi-lustred painting
Designed and made by Joel
Philip Myers, USA

192, 193
Glass panel, square hand-blown
elements, acquamarine/blue
glass; 32×32 (12½″×12½″)
(detail)
Designed by Raoul Goldoni and
made at Rogaška Glasfactory,
Yugoslavia

192

193

194

195

194, 195
Glass mural, composed of 310 cylindrical elements; the image changes its colour and shape according to position of viewer and reflection of light; 2·70 ×2 (8′ 3½″ ×6′ 6″)
Designed and made by Stanislav Libenský and Jaroslava Brychtová for the Czechoslovak Embassy in Stockholm, at Železnobrodské sklo np, Czechoslovakia

196
Decorative panel, fused glass;
2·25 m (6′ 6″) high
Designed and made by
Stanislav Libenský and
Jaroslava Brychtová, for the
Prague Parliament, at Železno-
brodske sklo np, Czechoslovakia

197
Sculptures, cut clear lead glass
in four pieces; 17×17×17
($6\frac{1}{2}$″ × $6\frac{1}{2}$″ × $6\frac{1}{2}$″)
Designed and made by Marian
Karel, Czechoslovakia

198
Environmental composition,
glass sculptures on mirror
Designed and made by Erwin
Eisch, West Germany

197   198

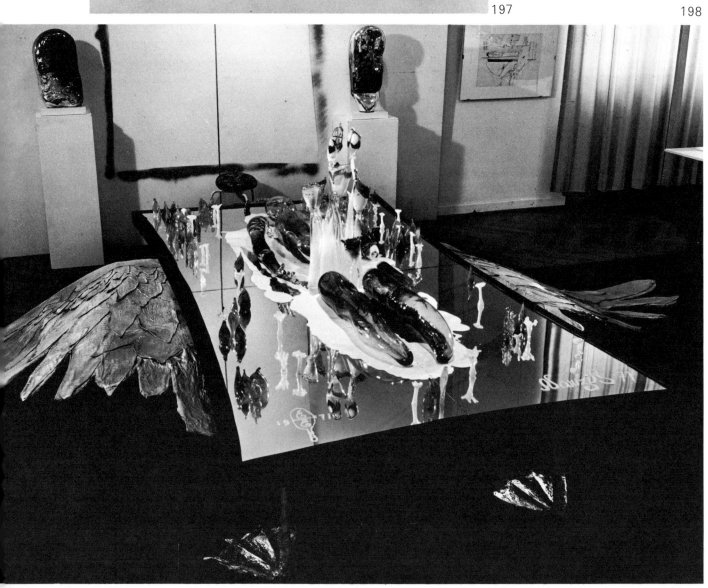

199
'Untitled Form', hot tooled,
dark amber glass with silver
nitrate optic patterns; 31·5
(12¾") high
Designed and made by Joel
Philip Myers, USA

200
'Pearlised Form', violet glass;
35·5 (14") high
Designed and made by Michael
Brown, England

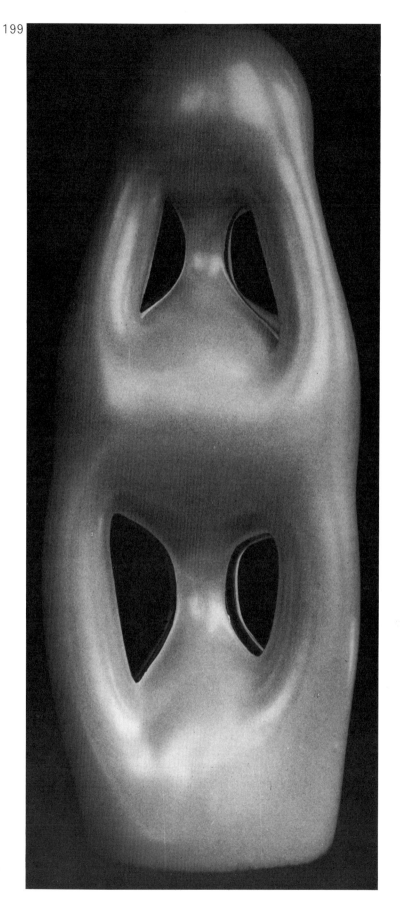

199

200

201
Form 1B, free blown silvered
glass
Designed and made by Sam J
Herman at the Royal College
of Art, London

Trends in
furnishing
and Decorative art

205 *Opposite*
'Podium 3' furniture programme;
plinths of various sizes and
heights, cabinets and special
'lamella' mattresses will
combine in different ways; ash
lacquered white/grey frames;
platforms and cabinets in sand
or green velour finish, yellow
or black stained
Designed and made by
Interlübke, West Germany

203
'Savings Fish', porcelain,
underglaze decoration, gold or
cobalt blue on white
Designed by Anne-Marie
Ødegaard for Porsgrunds
Porselaensfabrik A/S, Norway

202
'Peota' chair, knockdown
construction, natural ash or
glossy black finish
Designed by Gigi Sabadin for
Stilwood, Italy

204
'Toco' bed, black or white
lacquered wood, chrome steel
support; 2 m × 1·70 m
(6' 6" × 5' 7")
Designed by Ennio Chiggio
for Zoarch, Italy

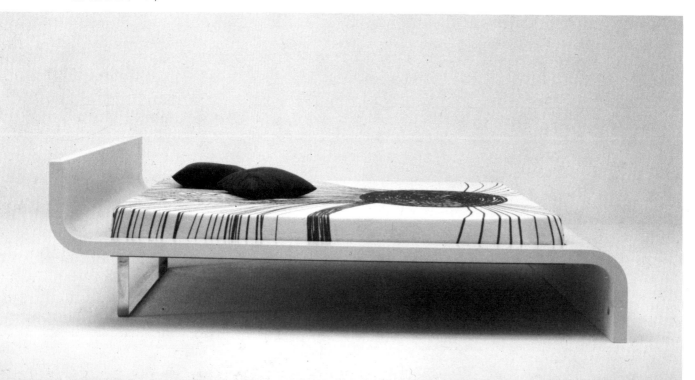

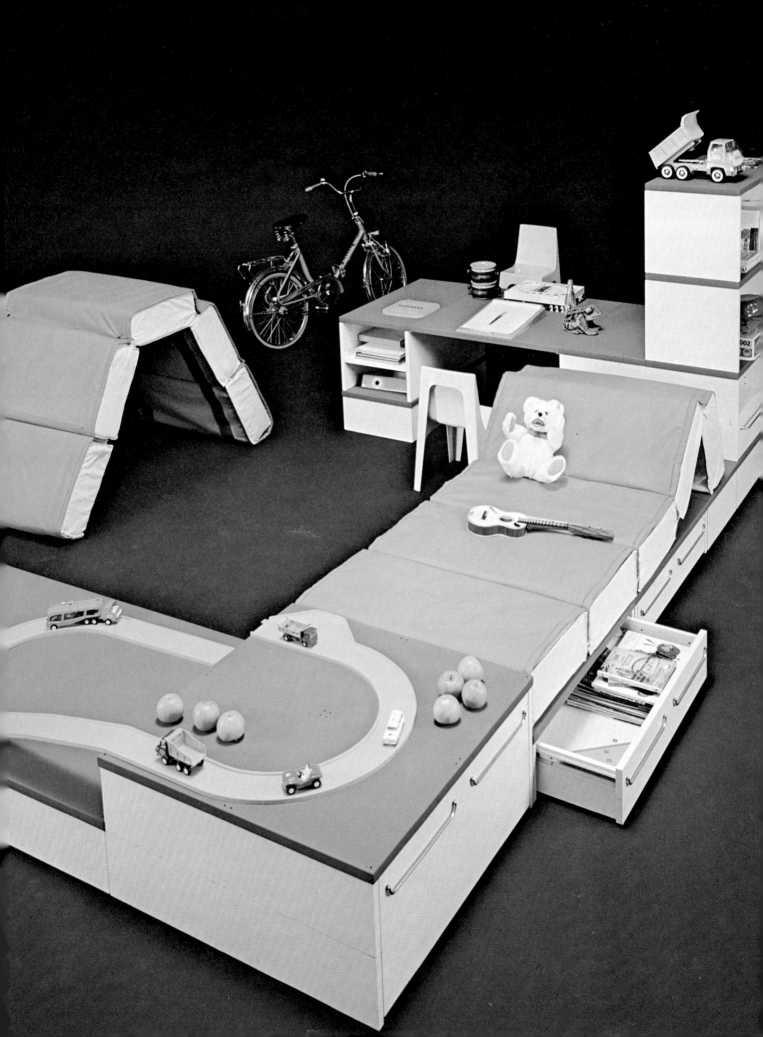

206
'Beaujardin' print, sheer curtain
material or heavy textured linen
for wallcovering; four colourways, 60" pattern repeat
Designed and made by Elenhank
Designers Inc, USA

207
'Maggiolina' stainless steel
frame, black leather 'sling',
seat and cushions covered
with Vistram, cloth, suede or
leather; 71×102×37
(28"×40"×14½")
Designed by Marco Zanuso for
Zanotta SpA, Italy

208
'Fortuna', polyurethane table,
red, white, black, brown,
orange, yellow or green;
1 m×1 m×37 (39½"×39½"×
14½")
Designed by Rolf-Erik Nyman
for HT-Collection, Finland

209
'Westlake' suite, lounge chair
and ottoman, chrome tubing,
cushions covered with proofed
nylon
Designed by Jerry Johnson for
Landes, USA

210
Bed tray with collapsible
supports, white or red Vedril;
58×35×23 (22¾"×13¾"×9")
Designed by Luigi Massoni for
Fratelli Guzzini, Italy

211
'Tai' bed, ash frame stained
natural or smoke, white and
blue heavy cotton mattress and
bolster cover; 2·46 m×2·12 m×
33 (8'×6' 10¾"×13")
Designed by R Pamio and
R Toso for Stilwood, Italy

212
'Sirio' table lamp, two Vedril
structures are assembled by
screws; white or white/orange
Designed by E Lampa and
S Brazzoli for Harvey Guzzini,
Italy

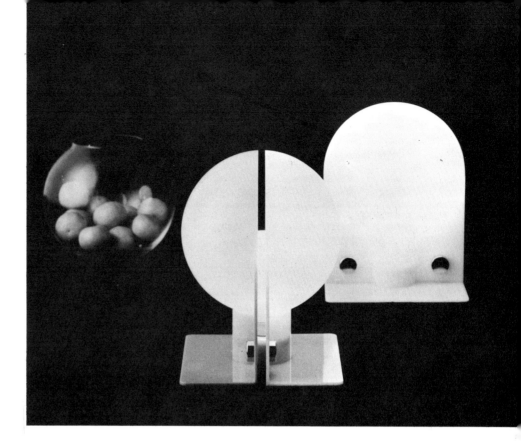

213
'Lounge' stitched brown fabric
filled with shredded foam;
1·7 m×51 and 45·5×51
(42"×20" and 18"×20")
Designed and made by
Geraldine Ann Snyder, USA

214
System furniture comprising
storage cupboard, shelves and
revolving bed units; complemented by Dekostoff curtains/
roller blinds and matching
carpeting (not shown); folding
chair is finished in colours
matching Dekostoff material.
Designed and made by
Interlübke, West Germany

215
Wardrobe illustrated on left
combines with 'Environment
121', freestanding storage units
enclosing particular areas;
specially designed Dekostoff
material covers sofa/bed and
wall
Designed and made by
Interlübke, West Germany

216
Book ends, obtained by
folding a single sheet of silver
plated metal; 21×21 (8¼″×8¼″)
Designed by Lino Sabattini for
Argenteria Sabattini, Italy.

218
'Encore', knock down record
storage components can be
added in pairs to basic unit of
four; smoke grey and white,
with optional nylon castors;
injection moulded styrene;
37×41×33 (14½″×16″×13″)
Designed by Frank Height and
Frank Guille for Artifact Design
Limited, England

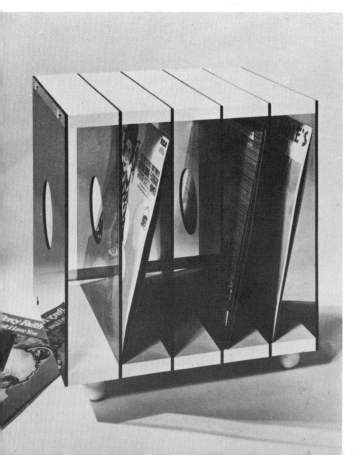

217
Fruit salad/Punch bowl, glass
with serving ladle, and
cover/stand, of silver plated
metal; 16·5 ×17 (6½″×6¾″)
Designed by Lino Sabattini for
Argenteria Sabattini, Italy

219

219, 221
'Blop', series of two-seater,
chair, stool and tables; wooden
frame with covered, steel
springs base, surfaces and
tables of ash plywood clear
varnished or black glossy
polyester; feet of injection
moulded Moplen, non-slip
rubber stops; removable printed
velvet, leather or wool covers
Designed by Carlo Bartoli and
Fumio Okura for Giuseppe Rossi,
Italy

220
Coffee Pot, silver with juniper
wood handle
Designed and made by
Sigurd Persson, Sweden

220

221

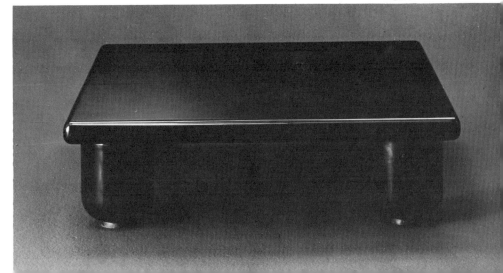

222
'Sesselprogramm 620', table,
containers and seating elements;
seating has low or high back
and can be used singly or in
combination of two or more by
means of a simple locking
device; tables and containers
are plastic, seating shells are
wood sprayed light grey, white
or black, with leather covered
cushions; excepting the tables
all components are fitted with
castors
Designed by Dieter Rams for
Wiese Vitsoe, West Germany

223
'Laotian Ikat'; the ancient Ikat
technique consists of wrapping
in pattern the silk weft, dyeing,
unwrapping and dyeing again
prior to weaving; pink/saffron
melange with gold metallic
guimpe
Designed by Jack Lenor Larsen
and hand-woven in Thailand
for Jack Lenor Larsen Inc, USA

223

224, 225
Table no. 66 and Chair no. 27,
laminated veneer maple clear
lacquered; table measures
1 m × 1 m × 30 (39¼″ × 39¼″ ×
11¾″), chair has metal and
rubber shock absorbing fitments
and is covered with leather,
seven colourways; 70 × 70 × 35
(27½″ × 27½″ × 13¾″)
Designed by Poul Kjaerholm for
E Kold Christensen A/S,
Denmark

225   224

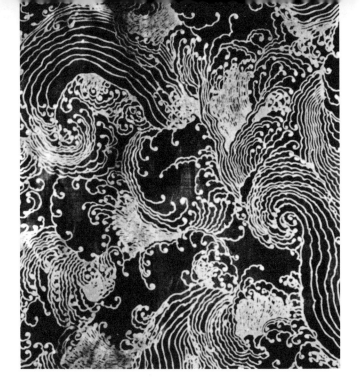

226
'South China Sea' hand printed
light or heavy weight silk, with
discharge dyes creating a
negative image in off-white on
coloured background; nine
colourways, 36" pattern repeat
Designed by Jack Lenor Larsen
and hand woven in Thailand for
Jack Lenor Larsen Inc, USA

227
'Elefante', seating elements of
various sizes can be combined
in different ways; steel frames
laid in polyurethane foam,
removable covers of hemp,
wool, cotton or leather
Designed by R Toso and
R Pamio for Stilwood, Italy

228
'Mango', cutlery service,
stainless steel
Designed by Nanny Still for
Hackmann Oy, Finland

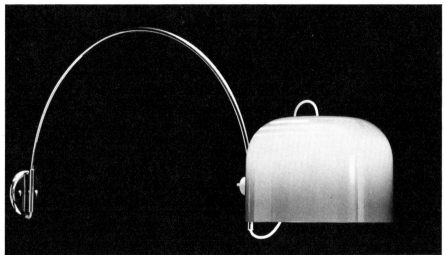

229
'Forma', wall lamp, chrome
structure and shade of white or
gold Vedril
Designed by Studio Tecnico
Harvey for Harvey Guzzini, Italy

230
'Polygon' porcelain coffee set,
white with blue stripes
Designed by Tapio Wirkkala for
Rosenthal, West Germany

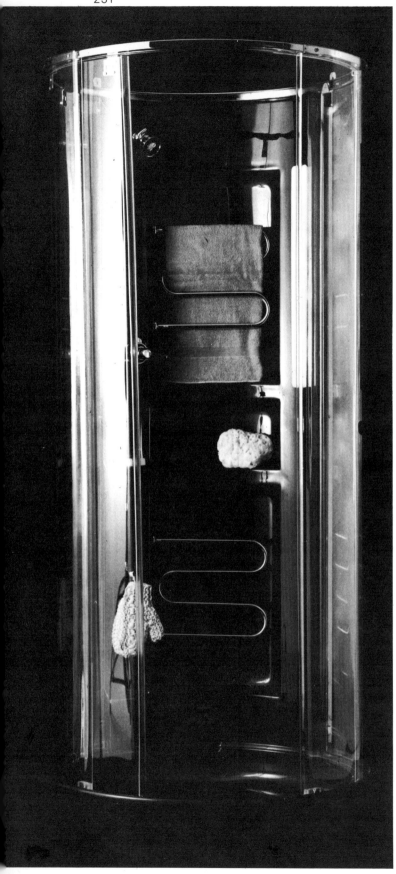

232

233

231
'Acquarius', cylindrical shower
unit includes heated towel rail
and fluorescent light tube in
screened recess; red or blue
ABS, 1 m (39$\frac{1}{4}$") diameter
2·10 m (6' 10") high
Designed by Fabio Lenci for
Teuco, Italy

232
'Spicchio', ceiling lamp; five
fan-shaped, white Vedril sheets
fold over a stainless steel
structure
Designed by E Lampa and
S Brazzoli for Harvey Guzzini,
Italy

233
'Mimosa' ceramic wall tiles,
brown on white
Designed by Sergio Asti for
CEDIT, Italy

234
'Arcadia', high back chair and
stool; chrome steel frame,
polyester cushions with proofed
nylon upholstery; 87·5×63·5×
43·5 (34$\frac{1}{2}$"×25"×17")
Designed by Byron Botker for
Landes, USA

234

235
'Conchiglia' table lamp, stove
enamelled frame holds white
Vedril shade and tray for small
objects; white, orange or red
frame; 36 (14¼") diameter 40
(15¾") high
Designed by L Buttura and
L Massoni for Harvey Guzzini,
Italy

236
'Rolls' armchair, foam padding
with leather or fabric upholstery
Designed by Sergio Asti for
Flexform, Italy

237

238

237, 238
Teapot, silver, handle and sliding lid of red Delrin, a hardwearing plastic normally used in industry for bearings
Overall height 18·7 (7¾″)
Designed by Alexandra McNeill for Peter Jones, England

239
Trolley, silver plated heavy metal with two crystal trays; 60×60× 60 (23⅝″ × 23⅝″ × 23⅝″)
On top tray, bottle and tumblers of glass with silver plated inserts
Designed by Lino Sabattini for Argenteria Sabattini, Italy

240
'Malibu' collection, waterproof
outdoor furniture; ABS
plumbing fittings, sling seats
with cushions covered of PVC
coated nylon, lemon, tangerine,
green or off-white
Designed by Heinz Meier for
Landes, USA

241
'Sunball', weatherproof sphere
houses folding seat, drinks shelf,
lighting and radio; can be
completely closed and locked
Designed by Günter Ferdinand
Ris for Rosenthal Einrichtung,
West Germany

242
Outdoor furniture, weather
proofed, steel knock down
construction; the table top is
yellow plastic laminate, the
covers are yellow and white
cotton stripes
Designed by Antonello Mosca
for Bieffeci, Italy

243
'Pierre Lumineuses', waterproof
outdoor lights; a mixture of
marble particles, silica and
polyester glue is mould-
blown by compressed air; the
resulting shapes are finished by
hand; natural stone colour in
six sizes
Designed by André Cazenave
for Atelier 'A', France

244
'Mobili nella Valle', chair
sculptures by Mario Ceroli for
Poltronova, Italy

245
'Trappola' coffee set,
mechanically extruded majolica,
hand formed, thin white glaze;
the set also includes jugs and
individual trays (not shown)
Designed and made by
Alessio Tasca, Italy

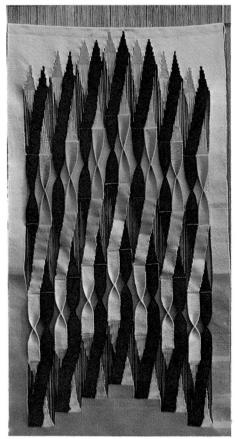

246

247

248

246
Double cloth tapestry, yellow,
black and white wool;
1·06 m × 1·98 m (42″ × 78″)
Designed and made by
Judith Poxson-Fawkes, USA

247
Hanging, glass and plastic
beads strung on nylon
monofilament, made on a loom;
91·5 × 2·43 m (3′ × 8′)
Designed and made by
Judith Poxson-Fawkes, USA

248
Hanging, spun, woven and
knotted wool; 1·24 m × 1·25 m
(48¾″ × 49″)
Designed and made by
Sophie Dawo, West Germany

249

249
'Symbolic Runner', serigraph,
from a limited edition series;
56×76·5 (22"×30")
Designed by Peter Max for
Peter Max Enterprises Inc, USA

250
'Livingcenter', four basic units
can serve many purposes;
a mobile recliner with side-trays
and compartments; a dining unit
with side flaps, pantry section,
containers and plate-warmer,
which can also function as a
desk; an outdoor/indoor service
unit; a wedge-shaped element
that becomes a seat or
head/back rest; black or white
upholstery
Designed by Joe Colombo for
Rosenthal Einrichtung, West
Germany

250

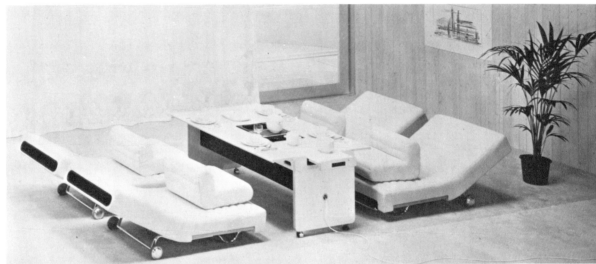

251

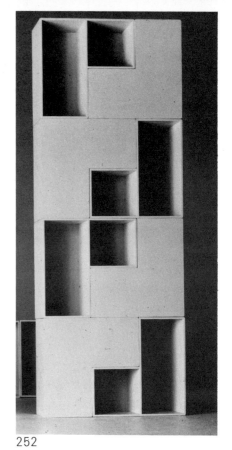

252

253

251, 252
'Dada', wedge shaped element can be assembled in endless variations to become free standing storage unit; stained wood or plastic
Designed by Kazuhide Takahama for Simon International, Italy

253
'Behr 1600 paneel' wall panelling of three heights and widths, on which various items of furniture can be hung by special hooks; white or brown
Designed by Product Design Jürgen Lange for Behr Möbel GmbH Production, West Germany

254
'Kimbo' coathangers and stands, laminated wood sprayed grey, white inside; stand tops and coat hooks are silver plated metal; 1·80 m, 1·50 m, 1 m and 60 (5' 10½", 59", 39½" and 23½")
Designed by Lino Sabattini for C A Nava, Italy

255
'Trim' table, a wooden half cube supports a square crystal top held in place by a metal clip, natural ash or black lacquer finish; 1·10 m × 1·10 m × 26 (43¼" × 43¼" × 10¼")
Designed and made by C A Nava, Italy

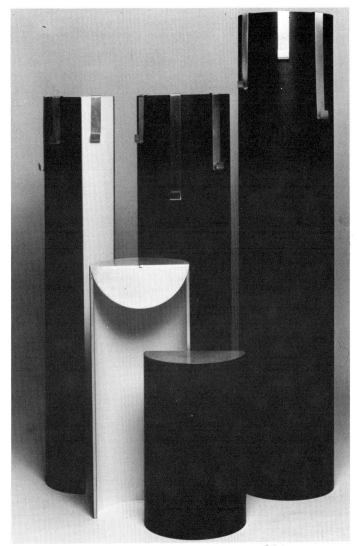

254

255

256
Bowl no. 0461, clay, apple
green reduction glaze with fire
marks and red iridescence;
21·5×10·5 (8½″×4⅛″)
Made by Gertrud and Otto
Natzler, USA
Max Yavno photograph;
courtesy of the Renwick Gallery,
National Collection of Fine Arts,
Smithsonian Institution

257
Closed Form no. 0428, clay,
dark green reduction glaze with
melt fissures and fire marks;
20×14 (7⅞″×5½″)
Made by Gertrud and Otto
Natzler, USA
Max Yavno photograph;
courtesy of the Renwick Gallery,
National Collection of Fine Arts,
Smithsonian Institution

256

257

258
Bowl, bone china, mould cast in
two layers, violet and white;
the decoration is hand carved
through the white to the violet
layer; 12 (4¾″) diameter
Designed and made by
Jacqueline Poncelet, England

259
'Goose Bowl', cast bone china,
hand-shaped and decorated,
transparent glaze; 6×12×6
(2⅜″×4¾″×2⅜″)
Designed and made by
Jacqueline Poncelet, England
Public collection: Veslandski
Kunstindustri Museum, Bergen

260
'Cylindrical Forms', hand thrown
glazed stoneware
Designed and made by Cyril
Smith for Doulton Studios,
Australia

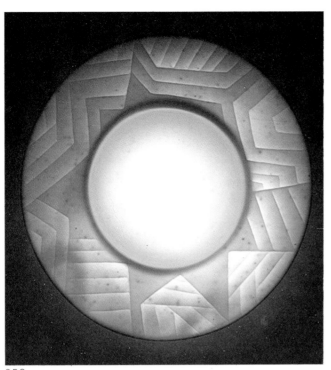

258

259

260

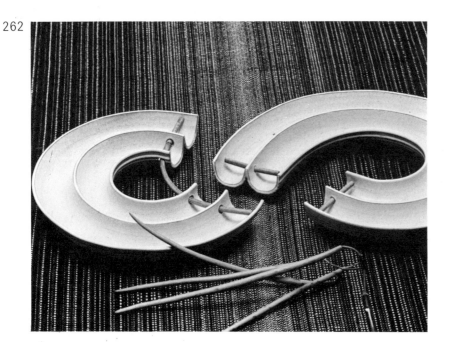

261
Interlocking egg, two piece
stoneware with porcelain egg
inside; salt glaze, 23 (9″) long
Made by Eileen Lewenstein,
England

262
Fruit holders, mechanically
extruded majolica cut and
shaped by hand, off-white thin
glaze; 65 × 35 and 40 × 25
(25½″ × 13¾″ and 15¾″ × 9¾″)
Designed and made by Alessio
Tasca, Italy

263
Porcelain bowl, hand thrown,
brown sgraffito and bronze;
10·5×20 (4$\frac{1}{8}$″×7$\frac{7}{8}$″)
Made by Lucie Rie, England

264
Cross handled bottle, ball clays
and sand with wood ash glaze;
22·5×19×23·5 (8$\frac{7}{8}$″×7$\frac{1}{2}$″×9$\frac{1}{4}$″)
Made by John Leach, England

263

264

265

266

267

268

265–268
'Elementi per una stanza vuota';
compact unit built of variable
components
Designed by Vico Magistretti
for Cassina, Italy

We would like to conclude this review of today's furnishing trends with three examples of how to fit an empty room. The solution offered by Egon Rainer is intended for an individual customer, the designs by Vico Magistretti and Luigi Massoni have evolved over a period of years to meet the practical demands of today's living, and are produced industrially.

With 'Furniture Components for an Empty Room', left, Vico Magistretti grouped into one unit three variable parts providing two beds, a cupboard, a worktop and a bookcase. The cupboard is shaped as a small staircase, by which the beds can be reached, the worktop can be lowered and doubles up as third bed; yet the whole unit measures only about 2 m × 2 m (6′ 6″ × 6′ 6″), leaving plenty of free space in a room of average size.

In 'Room for a Lady', below, Egon Rainer has given expression to a personal, essentially architectural, interpretation of space without overlooking its practical use; the bed rests on a platform which houses numerous containers for storage. Luigi Massoni, also preoccupied with space, develops the 'Cucinone', overpage, from his 'Casa con le Tasche' (see *Decorative Art in Modern Interiors* 1973/4, edited by Ella Moody, Studio Vista Publishers, p 69).

269

270

271

This 'Jumbo Kitchen' is much more than the name implies: a main free standing unit measuring 1·80 m×1·80 m×1·80 m (5' 10½"×5' 10½"×5' 10½") is fitted on one side as a compact kitchen complete with sink, cooking area, refrigerator, storage cupboards and shelves; on the other side a bed unfolds and glides on tracks along the inner walls. An optional complement to the 'Cucinone' is the 'Scalarmadio', literally 'Staircupboard', with a hidden wealth of storage containers (Fig. 270).

272

270–272
'Il Cucinone'; free standing unit comprising kitchen furniture, bed and storage cupboards
Designed by Luigi Massoni
for Boffi Arredamento Cucina
Italy

Manufacturers and Designers

Atelier 'A'
Lumière
4 Seymour Place
London W1H 5WF

Artifact Designs Limited
72 Boston Place
London NW1 6EX

Awashima Glass KK
3–11–6 Izumi Suginami-Ku
Tokyo 168

Bacci
via degli Ortolani 5
40139 Bologna
Italy

Fratelli Barbini
Murano
Italy

Behr Möbel GmbH Produktion
7317 Wendlingen
West Germany

William Bernstein
South Tow River
Box 73AA Rt 5
Burnsville
N C 28714
USA

Bieffeci
via V Arici 30
25010 San Polo (Brescia)
Italy

Boffi Arredamento Cucina SpA
via Padre Boga 31
20031 Cesano Maderno
(Milano)
Italy

Cassina
20036 Meda (Milano)
PO Box 102
Italy

Cedit
via de Amicis 44
Milano
Italy

Český Křišťál np
Chlum U Třeboně
Czechoslovakia

Elenhank Designers Inc
347 Burlington
Riverside
Illinois 11–60546
USA

Erwin Eisch
Bayr Wald
Frauenau
West Germany

Gral-Glashütte GmbH
7321 Dürnau
West Germany

Fratelli Guzzini
Recanati (MC)
Italy

Harvey Guzzini
via Le Grazie
62019 Recanati
Italy

Sam Herman
The Royal College of Art
Kensington Gore
London SW7

Holmegaard of Copenhagen
A/S
Norre Volgade 12
DK–1358 Copenhagen K

HT-Collection
Huonekalutuote
Lahti
Finland

Iittala Glassworks
14500 Iittala
Finland

Interlübke Möbelfabrik
4832 Wiedenbrück
West Germany

Peter Jones
Sloane Square
London SW1

E. Kold Christiensen
Rygards Alle 131
DK 2900 Hellerod
Denmark

Kosta Glasbruk Ab
Åforsgruppen
S-306 52 Kosta
Sweden

Landes Manufacturing Co
PO Box 2197 Gardena
California 90247

John Leach
Muchelney Pottery
Muchelney, nr Langford
Somerset
England

Royal Leerdam Glassworks
PO Box 8
Leerdam
Holland

Glashütte Leichlingen GmbH
D-7325 Boll
West Germany

Eileen Lewenstein
5 Belsize Lane
London NW3 5AD

Marvin Lipofsky
1012 Pardee
Berkeley
California 94710
USA

Richard Marquis
c/o Carl McCarthy
1359 Glendale Avenue
Berkeley
94708 California
USA

Joel-Phillip Myers
RR 2, Bunn St Road
Bloomington
Illinois 61701
USA

Peter Max Enterprises Inc
325 East 75th Street
New York, NY 10022

Cesare Augusto Nava
via de Amicis 1
20053 Desio (Milano)
Italy

Ab Orrefors Glasbruk
38040 Orrefors
Sweden

Poltronova srl
Agliana (Pistoia)
Italy

Jacqueline Poncelet
3 Kendoa Road
Clapham
London SW4

Judith Poxson Fawkes
9233 SW 8th Drive
Portland, Oregon 97219
USA

Egon Rainer
The Royal College of Art
Kensington Gore
London SW7

Riihimäen Lasi Oy
Riihimäki
Finland

Rogaška Glasfactory
Rogaška
Yugoslavia

Rosenthal AG
8672 Selb/Bayern
Postfach 104
West Germany

Giuseppe Rossi
Albizzate (Varese)
Italy

Argenteria Sabattini
via A Volta
22072 Bregnano (Como)
Italy

Livio Seguso
Murano
Italy

Simon International
via Emilia Levante 275
40068 San Lazzaro di Savena
  (Bologna)
Italy

Sirrah srl
via Callegherie 31
40026 Imola (Bologna)
Italy

Cyril Smith
Doulton Potteries
176 Victoria Avenue
Chatswood NSW 2067
Australia

Geraldine Ann Snyder
1387 Willow Drive
Louisville
Kentucky 40213
USA

Stilwood Sas
via Volturno 117
41032 Cavezzo (Modena)
Italy

Alessio Tasca Ceramiche
via Roberti 15
36055 Nove (Vicenza)
Italy

Teuco Sa
Montelupone (MC)
Italy

Venini SpA
Fondamenta Vetrai 50
30121 Murano
Italy

Oy Wärtsilä Ab Arabia
Hameentie 135
00560 Helsinki 56
Finland

Zanotta SpA
via Vittorio Veneto 57
20054 Nova Milanese
Italy

Zoarch
via Paganella 23
22063 Cantú (Como)
Italy